AUTHORITY RELATIONS AND ECONOMIC DECISION-MAKING IN VIETNAM

NORDIC INSTITUTE OF ASIAN STUDIES
Recent studies of Vietnamese history and society

Common Roots and Present Inequality: Ethnic Myths among
Highland Populations of Mainland Southeast Asia
Claes Corlin

Foreign Direct Investment and Economic Change in Vietnam:
Trends, Causes and Effects
Carolyn Gates and David Truong

Thailand and the Southeast Asian Networks
of the Vietnamese Revolution, 1885–1954
Christopher E. Goscha

Vietnam or Indochina? Contesting Concepts of Space
in Vietnamese Nationalism, 1887–1954
Christopher E. Goscha

Vietnam in a Changing World
Irene Nørlund, Carolyn Gates and Vu Cao Dam (eds)

Profit and Poverty in Rural Vietnam:
Winners and Losers of a Dismantled Revolution
*Rita Liljeström, Eva Lindskog,
Nguyen Van Ang and Vuong Xuan Tinh*

AUTHORITY RELATIONS AND ECONOMIC DECISION-MAKING IN VIETNAM

AN HISTORICAL PERSPECTIVE

Dang Phong
and Melanie Beresford

NIAS

Authority Relations and Economic Decision-Making in Vietnam
An Historical Perspective
by Dang Phong and Melanie Beresford

First published in 1998
by NIAS Publications
Nordic Institute of Asian Studies (NIAS)
Leifsgade 33, 2300 Copenhagen S, Denmark
Tel: (+45) 3254 8844 Fax: (+45) 3296 2530
E-mail: books@nias.ku.dk
Online: http//nias.ku.dk/books/

Typesetting by NIAS
Printed and bound in Great Britain by
Biddles Ltd, Kings Lynn and Guildford

NIAS Report series, No.38

ISBN 87-87062-65-8

Contents

Preface

This monograph was written as part of the Australian Vietnam Research Project in collaboration with the Economics Association of Vietnam. The overall objective of the project was to study the process of economic transition in Vietnam since the late 1970s. During the course of this research, we began to feel that a paper analysing the way the Vietnamese economic policy-making apparatus had developed over time would both fill an important lacuna in the existing literature and assist us in understanding the political processes at work during the transformation of the economic system. The present work is therefore the product of many discussions, draftings and redraftings, in which we drew on our collective experience as well as both empirical and theoretical sources which are too numerous to be cited here. We both hope that this first product of our collaboration will not be the last.

Because of some specific features of the Vietnamese decision-making process, we have had to rely largely on the methods of oral history. Researchers on Vietnam understand only too clearly that reliance on documentary sources to support one's arguments and analyses, especially on official decrees and documents, is likely to produce contrary results. One will not be able to understand the hidden truths within the process since, in most cases, the official documents simply do not reflect the real relations involved. To date, for example, there is still no official written recognition that the policy of reforming private capital in the North during 1956–57 and in the South during 1977–78 was erroneous. Throughout the period from 1959 to 1979, no official document or newspaper editorial said that cooperative agriculture in Vietnam was inefficient, at an impasse, and a mistake. Instead they reported the unremitting progress of the cooperative economy. In this study, therefore, we have relied heavily on our own observations, on unofficial documents and on interviews. Many who have worked or are still working within the political structure are unable to write about their experiences, but they may be prepared to speak about it in confidence. It is a fact of life in Vietnam that the truth is often without hard evidence, but the hard evidence is also often without truth.

Much of the primary source material for this essay is provided from the personal observations of the Vietnamese political system by Dang Phong over a period dating from the 1950s, as well as numerous interviews with state officials conducted by both authors and documentary sources belonging to the archive of the Institute of Economics, our personal collections and the published record such as the *Công Báo* (the government gazette). In most cases we have not been able to cite the sources individually.

The essay constitutes to some extent an eyewitness account. Dang Phong grew up in the midst of the Vietnamese revolution. His father was a high civil servant of the Democratic Republic of Vietnam (DRV) government during the resistance war against the French and his father-in-law was a leading member of the Viet Minh and also a government minister during the first 15 years of the Republic (see Le Van Hien 1995). After studying at Hanoi University in the 1950s, Dang Phong joined the Economics Institute of the then Social Sciences Commission in 1960, eventually becoming head of the Economic History Department. He also worked as a journalist during the war and, for a brief period after 1975, for the Committee for Transformation of the Commerce and Industry of the South, before moving to the Government Price Committee as a researcher and deputy editor of its journal. In 1995 he returned to the Economics Institute as a Senior Researcher and Director of the official research project on 'Fifty years' development of the Vietnamese economy'. He is now also Dean of Economics at the newly-formed Hanoi University of Business and Management. Although not a Party member, he is an occasional contributer to *Nhân Dân* (the official Party organ) and other newspapers. Throughout his career, he has worked close to senior policy advisers of Party and government leaders, with a multitude of opportunities to observe the system at work.

Melanie Beresford is a Senior Lecturer at Macquarie University in Sydney. Her association with academic research on Vietnamese political economy began nearly twenty years ago and, since then, she has completed a PhD at the University of Cambridge on the economic consequences of national unification and published two books and a large number of articles in international journals.

The interviews we have conducted, individually and together, have been with a wide range of people including former ministers, a former deputy prime minister, current and former senior civil servants, provincial Party secretaries, provincial heads of department, members of central Party committees, policy advisers, enterprise directors and fellow researchers. Documentary sources have been used, wherever possible, to supplement these oral sources. However, as mentioned above, the documentary sources need to be used with caution and, in any case, they tend to present the results rather than the process of decision-making. For those who want to study the process itself, oral sources, as well as the handful of published memoirs which are beginning to appear, are usually the only ones available. We hope and expect that as more information becomes available, the findings of the present paper will be receive both critical challenges and further development.

We would like to thank the Australian Research Council for funding and Stein Tønnesson for his comments on an earlier version of the manuscript. Melanie Beresford would also like to thank the director and fellows of NIAS for a stimulating two weeks spent there during the early stages of this research.

Introduction

In order to understand the role of the state in the economic transition in Vietnam we need first of all to gain an understanding of the way the political system has operated in the past. We need to find answers to questions such as: what are the political traditions on which new, or revamped, state institutions are being founded? Given that the Communist Party still rules, what are the continuities in the way the political system functions and to what extent has rapid social change altered the authority relations and decision-making processes in fundamental ways? The best way to achieve this is to treat the Vietnamese political system as a normal one in which the objectives and understanding of the issues by leading personalities, competition for leadership positions, advocacy of particularistic goals of social and state institutions, hierarchical processes and expressions of interest by various social groups, all have a role to play. Such an approach stands in contrast to what, in the past, has been the dominant western, especially American, approach of viewing communist-led states as 'totalitarian' or 'bureaucratic authoritarian' (Porter 1993) and looking at decision-making processes in terms of 'Kremlinology'[1] (that is, focusing on who, among the leading personalities, seems to be making the decisions and who is standing in the wings manoeuvring to take their place).

The result of looking at the Vietnamese system as operating according to similar principles as other systems is that we can see two things. Firstly, the system appears more democratic than what is portrayed in the 'totalitarian' and 'bureaucratic authoritarian' models. This aspect helps to explain the apparent flexibility of the Vietnamese political system in the face of rapid economic transition, as well as strengths and weaknesses in the democratisation process. Secondly, we can identify those characteristics which are peculiar to communist-led states and which make Vietnam less likely to move towards liberal models of democracy.[2]

Undoubtedly, the range of sources used for this essay give the material a rather 'top down' bias. What are largely missing from the picture are the responses of the population to major policy decisions and the way in which these responses provided inputs to the decision-making process itself. What we can see, however, is that policy did respond to popular sentiment, even if in a rather *ad hoc* and uncertain manner. There were few formal channels for the overt representation of popular interests and this contributed to the relatively slow pace of change at the formal policy level over time. Among the factors influencing the process, however, were the fundamental legitimacy of the Vietnamese state and the broadly accepted need for consensus within the political system. At different points in time this influence could operate in either a reformist or conservative direction. It is often remarked that, in socialist countries, the room for divergent expressions of interest is very limited and that certain taboos exist. However, in Vietnam we believe that the most fundamental taboo has been one which even the highest leaders have had to respect, and that is not to press against the interests of the people. Vietnamese political culture does not permit the survival of political regimes which sit on the people (Dang Phong 1997).

The development of the Party-state in Vietnam can be divided into three broad historical phases: (1) the period from

1945 to 1955, that is from the August Revolution to the Geneva Accords and establishment of the Democratic Republic in the northern half of the country; (2) the period from 1955 to 1986, mainly coinciding with the ascendancy of Le Duan to the position of General Secretary of the Party and, as well, the period of introduction, consolidation and disintegration of the central planning system; (3) the period of *đổi mới* after the 1986 Sixth Party Congress to the present. In what follows we shall consider the main developments in the political system of these three periods.

NOTES

1. See for example, Honey (1962) and Thai Quang Trung (1985) who attempted to identify factions within the leadership. For a critique see Beresford (1988: 88). Porter, among others, has proposed a 'consensus' model which seems more accurate, but remains focussed on ways of resolving differences within the elite (Porter 1993 115–116; Duiker 1995: 104).

2. For a discussion of an alternative way of looking at the process of democratisation in Vietnam, one which focusses on the idea of *substantive* rather than *formal* democratic forms, see Beresford and Nørlund (1995).

1

Establishment of the DRV Institutions

1945–55

The period 1945 to 1955 saw the early institution building of the Democratic Republic, based on an essentially private economy, combining elements of subsistence agriculture and market, in which state ownership as yet played a very small role. Although the kernel of the regime comprised the Viet Minh and Communist Party, the composition of society as a whole played an important role in determining the structure and policies of the state. The period can be divided into three distinct sub-periods: the early phase of establishing an independent government prior to the breakdown of relations with France in December 1946, the first stage of the resistance war and the later stages (from 1950 onwards) in which substantial international assistance became available to the DRV following diplomatic recognition by the Soviet Union and China.

In the first phase, the emphasis was very much on nation-building and consolidating the legitimacy of the newly formed state. The provisional government, elected by the national congress held at Tan Trao on 16–17 August, consisted of 14 people, of whom seven were neither Communist Party nor Viet Minh members.[1] The provisional government was reorganised on 1 January 1946, but this second government was in turn replaced after the election of the first National

15

Assembly which appointed Ho Chi Minh as President. His new government of 18 members, announced at the first meeting of the National Assembly on 2 March 1946, included ten who did not belong to the Party.[2] The inclusion of such a high number of non-Party ministers does not indicate, however, that the system of appointments was less under the influence of the Party than in later periods. Ho Chi Minh's inclusion of these people was largely tactical: it was aimed at achieving a climate of national reconciliation, to head off the potential for further internal upheavals at a time when the regime was under external threat due to the presence in the country of Guomindang and French troops. There was also the need to present the regime in a moderate light in order to try to win international recognition (Huynh Kim Khanh 1982).

Nevertheless, these non-Party ministers played an important role until the end of 1946. In this first year the government, rather than the Party, was the key apparatus of the Vietnamese state and showed unity of purpose in economic management under very trying circumstances. Soon after the provisional government had been established, Ho Chi Minh had declared that the country faced three main enemies and three main dangers: hunger, ignorance and foreign aggressors (*giặc đói, giặc dốt, giặc ngoại xâm*). The first danger, and the first priority, was famine relief, for which the mobilisation of Viet Minh units was vital, after which economic policy concentrated on developing production, stabilising prices, supplying of necessary goods to government bodies and the army, and the struggle against the power of foreign currencies.[3] A Committee to Build the Nation comprising both Party and non-Party experts provided policy advice.

In November, at a time when war had already broken out in the South, the Party issued an order proclaiming the ideology of 'resistance and nation building', signifying that the two problems of war and planning for economic construction were in fact two sides of the same coin. Survival against foreign aggression and economic construction were never considered as separate tasks, but were bound together in the thinking of the DRV leadership from the start. The second meeting of the National Assembly a year later was renamed the Resistance and Nation Building Assembly by Ho Chi Minh. In his *Thi đua ái quốc* (Patriotic Emulation) of June 1948, Ho reiterated his view that economic and resistance issues were inseparable (VNTKKC 1997: 34, 89, 169).[4]

Also contributing to the widespread acceptance of the regime during this period was the fact that the selection criteria for cadres in the state apparatus, from ministerial level to the workers, were ability, experience and patriotism. One of the main characteristics of the period was the wide use of experts and intellectuals in positions of responsibility. Provided that they adhered to the regime, relatively few obtained jobs on the basis of their political affiliation: most of those who did were members of the Nationalist Party (*Quốc Dân Đảng*), there due to the policy of national solidarity and approved by the National Assembly on Ho Chi Minh's personal insistence, despite the fact that they had not been elected.[5] Many civil servants from the colonial state apparatus were retained because of their experience. This was indeed a necessary measure given the shortage of expertise in the country. Few Vietnamese had had the opportunity, under the colonial regime, to gain positions of real responsibility and the new government had little choice but to use what talent was available. During his years of exile, Ho Chi Minh had spent much time studying the organisation of state machineries and national administration and, although he himself had no practical experience of these things prior to the revolution, he used these talented people well, whatever their background.

At the local level too, the new government showed great skill in mobilising influential personalities, especially teachers, into government service, while commencing the task of building up the Party's own local infrastructure.[6] At the time of the August Revolution, the Party had only some 5,000 members across the country and so relied heavily on its unifying and integrating policies to consolidate the legitimacy of the new state as well as its own presence within the state.

In the capital, people were amazed that a revolutionary government, grown up in the mountains and forests of the Viet Bac, proved itself adept at resolving so many complicated issues. Production, which had been in a state of crisis during the final stages of World War II, was stabilised within a few months. Living conditions were gradually restored from the tragic conditions of famine in the final year of the war.

Under the new government, trade was on the whole free and private entrepreneurs were encouraged in restoring production and getting transport, communications and industrial enterprises restarted. The harsh taxes of the colonial period were reduced. Despite very straitened public finances, efforts were made to help the peasants to restore production, through building dykes and repairing irrigation works. Ho Chi Minh's government displayed a neutral attitude towards peasants and landlords, issuing a communique in November 1945 which reduced rents by 25 per cent, prohibited the avoidance of rent payment, protected the property rights of landowners, made the People's Committees responsible for punishing violations of this decree, and gave them the role of mediators between landlords and peasants (VNTKKC 1997: 31). A system of economic governance was established through creation of a hierarchy of economic organs, from ministry to local departments. There was a strong emphasis on respect for the law in economic matters.

The French attack on Hanoi in December 1946 changed the situation dramatically and economics now came second to military matters in the priorities of the new Vietnamese government. The war ravaged a considerable part of the basic productive capacity and created instability in living conditions. There was also the problem of recruiting a large number of people for the army. Yet all through these years of resistance the system of economic management established during 1946 played a key role in guaranteeing the material conditions for the resistance to succeed, mainly through the distribution of goods for the government, army and population. One of the most noteworthy characteristics of this system was the high degree of delegation of authority within the heirarchy. Due to the difficulties of operation and communication under conditions of guerrilla warfare and with poorly developed infrastructure, local authorities necessarily had a large amount of discretion in applying central policies. This discretion was important because it allowed good local leaders to maintain popular support and mobilisation for the war effort by adapting policy to local conditions.

The most important of the state bodies in the field of economic management was the Ministry of Economy, which maintained a system of bureaux at all regional, provincial and district levels. An Economic Committee at the central government level, and comprising a number of the country's most experienced economists, was also established to draft policy proposals. However, the shortage of real economic expertise was glaring. It was not until after the establishment of diplomatic relations with China and the USSR in 1950 and the official opening of the Chinese border that thousands of young Vietnamese began to be sent north for training. Most went to the military school in Guilin, or the teacher training school in Nanning, especially established for the Vietnamese. But many others went directly into Chinese universities, sometimes on the basis of perhaps nine or ten years of schooling. When they returned to Vietnam in the mid-1950s, they immediately went into leading positions in the state apparatus and in the fledgling state enterprise sector.[7]

Direct state involvement in the economy began to increase slowly, principally via the defence enterprises set up to manufacture weapons for the army. Besides these, a few other state enterprises were established, mainly to meet the needs of the state apparatus or defence (paper, office equipment, machinery, soap, matches, ink and garments).

However, the main thrust of state intervention at that time was still market regulation. Some measures were taken to assist farmers by reducing taxes in regions experiencing difficulties, and limiting and controlling rents. Many small capitalists in the resistance zone operated enterprises to meet consumer demand for such goods as paper, ink, textiles, soap and cigarettes. Markets in the zone were dominated by the private sector and largely free, except that due to French air attacks they had to be held at night. Between the French-occupied zone and the resistance zone, however, trade was controlled by the state through limitations placed on items considered non-essential for production, defence and basic consumption.

While the economic results were generally good considering the circumstances, it would be too much to expect that a relatively inexperienced government would avoid blunders altogether. In some localities during 1948–49 the policy of blockading the enemy was interpreted to include all sorts of agricultural products, which meant that farmers in the liberated zones could not find a market (for instance meat producers in the southern region could not sell to the cities, while areas in the Viet Bac found their market for forest products too restricted). However, within a year or two it was found that the free circulation of goods brought more benefit to the resistance areas than the blockade and the mistake was rectified. Again, in 1948, the Economic Committee proposed price controls on the free market. Within a few days of the measure the supply of goods to the market dried up and within a week the measure had to be rescinded.[8]

The day-to-day running of economic life was in the hands of the government during 1945–55, and was carried out with a reasonable degree of autonomy. In contrast to the following period, the Communist Party did not directly involve itself in management of the economy or the government apparatus. Rather, leadership was exercised through policy guidance and through strategically placed cadres within the government. The Party organisation was also rather compact in comparison to its subsequent development.

The main task of the Party centre was to provide analysis, education and guidance on the Party line to its members. Within the government apparatus, two bodies – the Viet Minh group and the Party group – were the main transmission belts for Party leadership. The Viet Minh group could be described as the public part of the Party and included leading Viet Minh members within the government, while the Party group was a similar organisation of Communist Party members.[9] Thus the Party did not have its own economic management apparatus, but carried this out *indirectly* via its cadres placed within the government. At the same time, both the law and the orientation of cadres' activities in office were derived from Party policy. It was a method of organisation which was both neat and highly effective.

This system was replicated at the local level. In addition, local Viet Minh and Lien Viet organisations assisted in propaganda and mobilisation work.

Figure 1 overleaf sketches the authority relations within the state apparatus of Vietnam during this period. In this model, one finds little overlap between the tasks and functions of Party and government. The government as well as chairmen and departmental directors at the regional (*liên khu*),

Figure 1: Structure of authority 1945–55

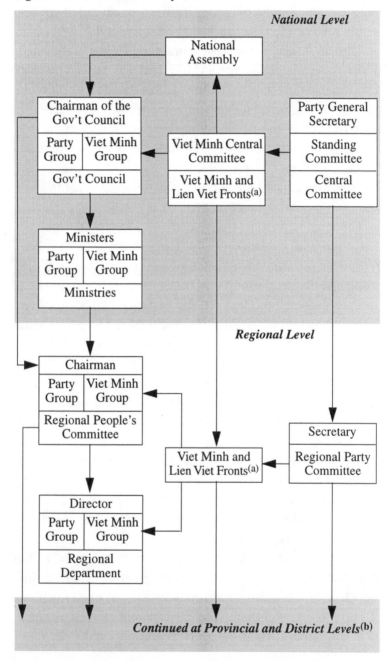

Continued at Provincial and District Levels(b)

Notes to Figure 1

(a) The Lien Viet Front (*Mặt trân liên hiệp quốc dân Việt Nam*) was formed in May 1945 to capture a wider range of people than were attracted to the Viet Minh with its well known links to the Communist Party. Leaders of both fronts were appointed by the Party and government, and their budgets came from the state budget. In 1950, for example, the government allocated 15 million dong to the Lien Viet. (Records of Government Council Meeting, May 1950, archives of Office of Government, 28 KT) In March 1951 the two fronts were merged and became known as Lien-Viet (VNTKKC 1997: 258).

(b) Government Decree no. 63 of 22 November 1945 established elected People's Councils only at the levels of commune and province. Administrative Committees were in turn elected by these Councils (*Công Báo* 1945, no. 11). However, in reality the composition of the Administrative Committees and, later, the Resistance and Administration Committees was decided by the level above.

provincial and district levels had real authority and responsibility in regulating the economy.

In relation to the role of the Communist Party, however, there were important differences over time. Shortly after the August Revolution, in November 1945, President Ho Chi Minh had formally declared the dissolution of the Indochinese Communist Party, aiming to create an atmosphere of social solidarity and, as mentioned above, a range of Party and non-Party people were included in the government. During this stage, the Party's role was carried out in secret. Indeed, it was not known as the 'Party', but by as the 'Organisation' (*Đoàn thê*). Members of the Organisation working in the state apparatus received Party orders and documents and read the Party newspaper, *Truth* (*Báo Sự thật*), in order to be able to do the work of the state as cadres of the state. At the head of this whole apparatus of Party *and* state was Ho Chi Minh.[10] Between 1947 and 1949, Ho ran four offices known as *Thận* (under Party Secretary, Truong Chinh); *Việt* (Hoang Quoc Viet, responsible for mass organisations); *Tô* (National Vice President and Deputy Prime Minister in charge of the government machinery, Pham Van Dong); *Văn* (Vo Nguyen Giap, in charge of the resistance). In this way Ho Chi Minh ensured his, and the Party's, leadership of the whole – the political, administrative, defence and popular mobilisation apparatuses.

By 1950, following the defeat in China of the Guomindang by the Communists and with American aid to the French in Vietnam increasing rapidly, the international situation had changed. Ho Chi Minh's attempt to maintain an equilibrium in relations with the Americans and the socialist bloc disintegrated. In January,[11] the DRV was accorded diplomatic recognition by the Soviet Union and China. Thereafter, having travelled overland in late January through China to the Soviet Union, Ho visited Moscow and Beijing in February and March to request aid (Ho Chi Minh 1994: 396–417). As a result of his trip, assistance to Vietnam's war effort, which had previously only trickled across the Chinese border, now became possible on a larger scale. It was also following this visit that the decision to send large numbers of young Vietnamese to China and the Soviet Union for training became possible (see p. 19 above).[12] These developments rendered ultimate victory more certain and later in the year, under pressure from Stalin and Mao, the Party decided to come out into the open as the Vietnam Workers' Party (VWP) at its Second Congress in early 1951. From then on, the role of the Party was manifested publicly and more clearly, even if its leadership of the state apparatus remained largely indirect.

In fact, it was only during 1951, with the arrival of large numbers of Chinese advisers in the fields of party organisation, economics and defence, that the Party line begin to shift towards more direct intervention and the role of the state in economic life begin to increase markedly through the establishment of state-run trade and the state bank and through preparations to mobilise the masses for land reform. From then on people from the landlord, bureaucratic and capitalist classes in the state machinery began to be noticed and gradually marginalised. The idea of the 'proletarian dictatorship' – this meant to the Vietnamese a workers' and peasants' dictatorship – began to emerge. Students, cadres and intellectuals were denounced, expelled, or gaoled by *ad hoc* people's courts. Class divisions reemerged in the villages, culminating in the land reform campaign of 1953–56. Those who had earlier contributed their wealth and efforts to the cause of independence, found themselves, with independence at hand, spurned and punished. Others who were insufficiently important to require punishment, began to worry and waver. Clearly, the land reform was associated with a rather heavy political purge.[13] One of its most important impacts was the destruction of old power bases in the villages, thereby increasing the capacity of the Party organisation to penetrate village society and mobilise the population to carry out its own programs later on.

Ho Chi Minh's own ideas during this time did not have the decisive significance that they had had during the August Revolution and early anti-French resistance, partly due to the growing strength and confidence in its organisational capacity of the Party as a whole and partly due to the growing significance of international influences. According to Hoang Tung, secretary of the Central Committee and head of the organisation committee for the Second Party Congress held in 1951, the Party centre decided to go for land reform, despite Ho Chi Minh's declaration that the procedures being advocated were too 'noisy'. Ho, however, bowed to the will of the majority.[14]

Nevertheless, there is evidence of some foot-dragging and procrastination by the Vietnamese in the face of international pressure to step up the pace of 'partification' of the state. For example, the Government Council meeting of December 1951 discussed an agenda essentially set by Stalin. The minutes recorded that

> [b]ased on three points concerning leadership put forward by Marshal Stalin, the Government Council reviewed its performance. ... The Government Council observed: 1) at the beginning of 1951 the government's program lacked concreteness and had not set out the main tasks for each period ... 2) there were many shortcomings in implementation; 3) organisation of the machinery for implementation of the program also contained shortcomings, as did the training of cadres.

At the same time, the question of land reform was relegated to number 11 on the agenda and only the question of ameliorating conditions of tenant farmers was dealt with. Land tenure was extended from three to five years and landlords who wished to claim land which had been cleared for cultivation by tenants must pay compensation.[15]

Again, in its meeting of August 1952, the Government approached the question of land reform cautiously, merely assigning the Party Economic and Finance Committees the task of carrying out research. It was not until March 1954, four years after Ho's visits to Moscow and Beijing, that a concrete plan for mobilising the masses for land reform, regulations governing the organisation of the Central Land Reform Committee and selection of the Committee were decided on.[16]

The errors associated with the land reform campaign were exposed in 1956, coinciding with events of the 20th Party Congress in the Soviet Union, and personal denunciations were stopped, leaving Vietnam with somewhat less onerous consequences than the similar events in neighbouring China. Vietnamese political culture, in any case, has more of a spirit of restraint and early recognition of injustice. Ho Chi Minh's role was very important here: his experiences with intellectuals abroad had led him to greater sympathy with them, and he was able to deflect some of the more extreme Maoist tendencies in Vietnam, even if, in the context of dependence on Chinese aid, he could not block them entirely.

After the 1951 Congress, with the open establishment of the VWP, the Party also had a more direct impact on the state machinery. It slowly came to decide not only the strategic goals of economic policy, but the concrete work of implementation. The government apparatus slowly lost its independence and people administering the state machinery took on a rather different role and position. Party Central Committee meetings marked this change as shown by the following plena:

- The first plenum, in March 1951, debated economic and financial issues such as the establishment of state trade, banking, and agricultural tax.
- The second plenum (October 1951) discussed internal strengthening, principally strengthening Party organisation in its new, more public role.
- The third plenum (April 1952) discussed the problem of rectification and re-education, and thus opened the period of very painful purges.[17]
- The fourth plenum (January 1953) was on the problem of land reform.
- The fifth plenum (November 1953) decided to proceed with land reform according to the Chinese model.

Thus during the anti-French resistance the tendency towards 'partification' of the state apparatus had already begun; a step was taken towards the machinery of government and legislature becoming the administrative organs of the Party. Certainly this change did not take place overnight, but the process was nevertheless discernible in the last years of the resistance.

In summary, then, we can say that the establishment of authority relations and decision-making processes during the first decade of the DRV's existence were characterised by an arms-length role for the Communist Party.[18] Under the difficult conditions of war and revolution, the need to rely on the skills and commitment of all strata of the population in order to maximise national unity was paramount in the organisational thinking of the revolutionary leadership, and of Ho Chi Minh in particular. The Party therefore tended to stand back, out of public view, preferring to wield its influence indirectly through the Viet Minh and Party groups and its members within the state apparatus. One should not deduce, however, that the Party was less powerful during this period than in the subsequent one, as is evident from Ho Chi Minh's ability to impose a tactical withdrawal in deciding on the composition of early governments, despite the over-whelming success of the Viet Minh in the 1946 election. It was only during the early 1950s, as independence became more assured and Chinese influence began to be felt more strongly, that a more orthodox socialist economic model began to be put in place and direct influence of the Party centre on policy and of the Party organisation in all spheres of administration could be increasingly observed.

Arguably the Communists gained enormous popular legiti-macy, not only from their early successes in the economic field but also from their victory in the anti-French resistance. The Party leaders could feel, with some justification, that their domestic and international policies reflected the wider national interest, despite the obvious difficulties, by 1955, of carrying the support of the minority strata of intellectuals, bourgeoisie and landlords. Nevertheless, the confidence gained from the resistance stage of development of the DRV state laid the groundwork for the following period of 'socialist transformation'.

NOTES

1. Proclamation of the DRV government, 28 August 1945, *Công Báo* no. 1, 29.9.45. The non-Party, non-Viet Minh members were: Minister for Youth, Duong Duc Hien; Minister of Economy, Nguyen Manh Ha; Minister for Social Affairs, Nguyen Van To; Minister for Justice, Vu Trong Khanh; Minister for Transport and Communications Dao Trong Kim; Minister for Education Vu Dinh Hoe; and Minister without Portfolio Nguyen Van Xuan.

2. *Công Báo*, no. 15, 13 April 1946: 204. The non-Party ministers were: Vice-President Nguyen Hai Than; Minister for Youth Affairs Duong Duc Hien; Minister for Economy Nguyen Tuong Long; Vice-Minister for Economy Nguyen Manh Ha; Minister for Social Affairs, Nguyen Van To; Minister of Justice, Vu Trong Khanh; Vice-Minister of Health Hoang Thich Tri; Minister of Transport and Communications, Dao Trong Kim; Minister for Education, Vu Dinh Hoe; and Minister without Portfolio, Nguyen Van Xuan. Seventy non-elected members of the Nationalist and another minor party were co-opted into the National Assembly at the same time.

3. The French franc, nationalist Chinese currency and the piastres of the Banque de l'Indochine were all in circulation.

4. After the August Revolution, People's Committees were established as the local authority. From November 1945, two sections were established, Administrative Committees, in charge of civilian matters including the economy, and Resistance Committees, set up first of all in the southern region and then throughout the whole country to mobilise the people and organise the resistance. The two committees were merged in October 1947 to form Resistance and Administration Committees. (*Công Báo*, 1947: 272)

5. This group remained formally in the government until just before the outbreak of war at the end of 1946, although following the departure of Guomindang forces, beginning in the summer of that year, and increasing repression of the party by the Communists, they had mostly fled to China or gone into hiding before any formal change of government. Some were arrested on criminal charges.

6. Among the few studies available in English on the local level politics of the period, Hy Van Luong (1992: 140–146) provides an account of the relationship between the new government and the population of Phu Tho province during 1945–46.

7. One of these individuals described to the authors how, newly graduated in transport economics, he had been sent to Hon Gai in 1955 to oversee the takeover of the coal mines from the French management. He and his team followed the French managers around for three months, writing down everything they did and, although unable to prevent the French from removing or destroying the mines' equipment, used this 'training' when they took over the mine. Vietnamese working at the mines before 1955 could not attain senior management positions, but were restricted to lower-level supervisory jobs (Guillaumat 1938: 1293).

8. Details of the economic history of this period can be found in Dang Phong 1991; Vo Nhan Tri 1963; and Doan Trong Truyen and Pham Thanh Vinh 1966.

9. Secretary of the Viet Minh group during the resistance period was Minister of Finance Le Van Hien. Secretary of the Party group was Vo Nguyen Giap.

10. In addition to his role as State President, Ho Chi Minh held the positions of Prime Minister (1945–55) and Party President (from 1951). He was also in charge of foreign affairs during the two provisional governments of 1945–46.

11. On 14 January 1950 (Viện Sử Học 1990: 50).

12. Record of Government Council Meeting, April 1950, archives of the Office of Government, 27 KT.

13. Vo Nhan Tri (1990: 2–7) cites a large number of Vietnamese Communist Party and other official sources on this, including the *Nhân Dân* report by Vo Nguyen Giap in October 1956, and the Economic Institute's comprehensive volume published in 1968 (Tran Phuong 1968). See also Hy Van Luong (1992: 159 and 186–194) for a local account.

14. The issue is difficult to judge in the absence of more thorough research. Such demands for radical land reform were not unusual in Southeast Asia at the time and there has been little argument with the Party's claim that its agrarian reform program met a genuine popular demand for security of land tenure and was particularly important in gaining support for the mobilisation of peasants for the military effort at Dien Bien Phu (Vo Nguyen Giap 1964; CPV 1980). Other regimes in the region which attempted land reform, in a context where land ownership remained the most important source of capital accumulation for the wealthy, generally

failed to achieve significant redistribution. However, it is not at all clear that the *Chinese-style* reform introduced from 1954 onwards achieved these results. Several authors have argued that the *method* of mobilisation for reform led to intense divisions within village society (Moise 1976; Gordon 1981; White 1983). Tran Phuong (1968: 191) points out that half the land distributed had in fact been distributed *prior* to the land reform proper. Moreover, Ho Viet Thang, vice-minister for agriculture and chair of the Central Land Reform Committee, reported to the Government in July 1954 (that is, *after* the signing of the Geneva Accords and *after* Dien Bien Phu) that the land reform had so far affected only 105,000 persons in two provinces (Thai Binh and Thanh Hoa).

15. The above points come from the Records of Government Council Meetings during the Resistance Period, archives of the Office of Government.

16. Records of Government Council Meetings during the Resistance Period, no. 059, p. 42

17. The second and third plena particularly reflected the increasing Maoist influence on Vietnamese politics which had begun to emerge as early as 1948 with the publication of Truong Chinh's *The Resistance Will Win* and the holding of a National Cultural Congress where the need for more class-oriented politics had been urged by the General Secretary.

18. A similar strategy was pursued in the southern half of the country after the formation of the National Front for the Liberation of the South in 1960 (Porter 1993: 20–21).

2

The Party State

1955–86

Looked at overall, this is the period of 'partification' of the state, when it gradually took on the character of a party-state. Whereas the earlier period can be seen as one of pragmatism, in which the very survival of the nation-state was uppermost in Party thinking, the period after the Geneva Agreement can be seen as one in which the 'transition to socialism' came to the fore. An essential ingredient of the 'partification' of the state which this transition implied was also the 'statisation' of the economy. In other words, implementation of the Communist Party's vision of creating a socialist Vietnam involved not only increasingly direct Party rule (the Party-state), but establishment of central planning and expanding state ownership and control of the means of production.

The model developed most fully after the Third Party Congress in 1960, but, as already noted, the tendency was apparent earlier. Even by 1955 the Central Committee was deciding the most important policy programs at its plenary conferences. Some of the major decisions of this period are listed below:

- The seventh, eighth and ninth plena (March and August 1955, June 1956) advocated unification of the country by peaceful means.

- The tenth plenum (August 1956) confirmed that there had been errors in the land reform and reorganisation and decided a plan of rectification.[1]
- The twelfth plenum (March 1957) discussed the state plan for 1957.
- The thirteenth plenum (December 1957) discussed improvements in the salary system.
- The fourteenth plenum (December 1958) advocated stepping up socialisation of agriculture, industry and trade.
- The fifteenth plenum (January 1959) received a very thorough report by Le Duan on the revolutonary situation in the south and decided to launch the armed struggle.
- The sixteenth plenum (April 1959) made two decisions on reform of agriculture and reform of industry and trade.

Party resolutions were no longer sketches of the line and the organisation needed to guide its implementation, but began to dictate day-to-day government administration.

As noted above, Ho Chi Minh's personal imprint was no longer as strong as it had been earlier. In relation to the two resolutions of the 14th Plenum on reform of agriculture and of industry and commerce, he emphasised strongly that it was necessary to 'stick to the principles of voluntary change, benefit to the people, the importance of quality and consolidation of results along the way'.[2] Despite his urging, peasants were frequently coerced into collectives by cadres charged with implementation and the reform of industry and commerce was done in a similar manner. A subsequent official evaluation of the results by the Party (in the *History of the Communist Party of Vietnam*) admitted that 'These instructions were neither specified nor deeply comprehended' (CPV 1995: 120). The book continued:

> General shortcomings of the socialist transformation of 1958–60 were haste, not having a firm grasp of good precepts, wanting to abolish immediately the multi-sectoral

economy ... the economy at this time already had defects demanding adjustment later on and should have been transformed at a level commensurate with productive capacity and the initial steps in a period of transition. (Ibid.: 129)

At the Third Party Congress in September 1960, with the election of a new Central Committee, Le Duan became General Secretary and the tendency to voluntarism in policy and diminution of the government's role increased. From now on the model typical of the Party-state became dominant and the state apparatus was more and more controlled by the corresponding Party organs. Government, ministries and directors not only answered to their superior levels, but *primarily* to the relevant Party committees. The Prime Minister's real power as head of government disappeared, though he remained influential through his Politbureau membership, and the actual functions of economic governance were taken over by the Party apparatus.

The National Assembly had acquired, by this time, more of a purely formal character – a legal secretary for the laws written by the Party – approving and promulgating the functions of government and localities. The role of the national President was also reduced. By the 1960s, Ho Chi Minh was already old and unwell.[3] He had delegated most of his Party and government work and become more of a national symbolic figure.

In what follows we shall attempt to demonstrate the structure of authority relations which prevailed from 1960 until the formal adoption of *đổi mới* in 1986. Figure 2 overleaf illustrates the system of relations between Party and government of this period which are elaborated further in the next three sections. Our objective is to draw out those factors which, on the one hand, enhanced the flexibility of the Party-state system, in the long run enabling it to adapt to conditions of fundamental change, and, on the other hand, slowed down the process of adaptation, rendering change difficult.

Figure 2: Structure of Party and state authority 1960–86

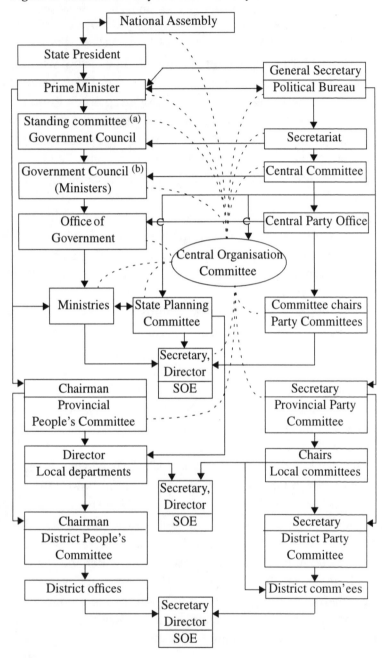

Notes to Figure 2

(a) Included the Prime Minister, the Deputy Prime Ministers and Minister for the Office of Government. In 1980, this last function was divided in two: (1) Secretary-General of the Office of the Council of Ministers who was a member of the Standing Committee, (2) the head of the Office of the Council of Ministers who was equivalent to a minister, but not a member of the Standing Committee.

(b) In 1981, the Soviet name of Council of Ministers (*Hội Đồng Bộ Trưởng*) was adopted. In October 1992, following the collapse of the Soviet Union, the name Government Council (*Hội Đồng Chính Phủ*) was restored (*Công Báo*, 1981: 279 and 1992: 522).

Key

lines of authority———▶   appointment by COC · - - - - - -

THE GOVERNMENT MACHINERY

The system of governmental organisation remained much the same as in the earlier period. The central body of government was the Government Council (*Hội Đồng Chính Phủ*)[4] which included the ministers and had a standing committee comprising the deputy prime ministers and Chairman of the Office of Government. Together these were led by the Prime Minister. Assistance to the Prime Minister, the standing committee and the Government Council was provided by the Office of Government. Under the government were what the Vietnamese term *branches* for which members of the Government Council (i.e. ministers) were responsible. Throughout this period the government included about 15–20 ministers.

Among the ministries, the State Planning Committee (SPC) stood higher than the others due to its overarching role in construction of the plan and coordination between branches, between centre and localities and between the various localities. It was under the charge of a deputy prime minister who was normally also a Politbureau member[5] and nominally accountable to the Prime Minister. In reality, however, the SPC was accountable less to the head of government than to the General Secretary, who himself participated in the construction of the plans, giving direct orders on setting norms and allocation of resources between branches and provinces. Though formally responsible, the Prime Minister was frequently unaware of these directives.

Below the central organs in the hierarchy were the provinces (by this time the regions had been abolished). Each had a standing committee of the provincial People's Committee made up of the chairman and deputy chairmen. Below these again were the directors of provincial departments, varying in number according to the province's situation and, lastly, the production enterprises and trading companies. At each level there was a parallel Party organisation. Within enterprises, for example, the director normally also held the position of deputy Party secretary, while the Party secretary was usually deputy director. Until the 1980s, it was the Party secretary, rather than the director, who was the final arbiter on problems of the production plan and the regime within the enterprise. East German and Soviet advisory teams on management reform, visiting Vietnam in the 1970s, commented that Party secretaries tended to interfere too much with the work of the directors.[6]

While the central, provincial and district levels shared a very similar organisational model, that of the lowest level, the commune (or in urban areas the precinct), was both simpler and more restricted. Each commune had a chairman and deputy chairman (often the Party secretary doubled as commune chairman) and several committee members in charge of areas such as security, social affairs (culture, education, health, welfare), agriculture and various branches of trade. Where the commune did not have a lot of sideline industries, then the person in charge of agriculture would usually take them on. Sometimes the commune committee would also have a secretary for everyday administrative problems.

Whether communes included one, two or three cooperatives, the cooperative economy was run by a management committee which accounted directly to the district level organs, while local administrative functions generally belonged to the commune People's Committee. As with the state enterprises, then, there was a certain division of economic and administrative functions at this level. Cooperatives did, in the 1960s and 1970s, undertake some work of an administrative nature. They had the powers to send cooperative members to school or to hospital, issue certificates or permit the transport of goods and buying or selling of materials for the cooperative. After the introduction of the contract system in 1981, however, the cooperatives gradually lost their role as the basic economic unit and the role of the commune People's Committees as the lowest level of state authority grew. Farmers' relations with the commune People's Committee are no longer normally carried out through the cooperative at all.

During the reform process, there were a number of shifts in the structure of government, particularly at the ministerial level. Since some sections of the bureaucy had a stronger interest in preventing or slowing the pace of reform than others, a device that could be used to overcome their objections was to restructure the ministerial apparatus, either through mergers which effectively eclipsed a conservative minister or through establishing new bodies.[7] This was the case with the merger of the Ministries of Domestic Trade and Food in 1980 and, subsequently the Ministries of Domestic and Foreign Trade in 1986. In both cases the more conservative of the two ministers was moved to a less powerful position.[8] In 1988, a new ministerial level body, the State Committee on Cooperation and Investment, was established following the passage of the Foreign Investment Law, to oversee the issuing of licences, thus removing a considerable part of the State Planning Committee's former power over foreign capital inflows.

THE PARTY MACHINERY

The 'Party centre' consisted of four major institutions, the Political Bureau, Secretariat, Central Committee and a series of specialised committees. At the highest level of the Party apparatus, forming the executive committee of the Central Committee, were the General Secretary and the Political Bureau, together constituting the most powerful group in the country. All basic policy programs were formed here and all the most important positions in government were inevitably held by Politbureau members. The President of the National Assembly, the Prime Minister, Chairman of the SPC, Foreign Minister, Ministers for Interior and Defence and, usually, the Party secretaries of Hanoi and Ho Chi Minh City (after 1975) were all members of this elite organisation.[9]

The inner workings of the Politbureau during this period will probably never be fully understood, but an example taken from the period 1960–76, when Le Duan was at the head of the Party, may serve to demonstrate that it was by no means a one-man show. People often observe that Le Duan infrequently went to Politbureau meetings, but preferred to work with experts or else with a handful of Politbureau members. They are therefore tempted to say that he was dictatorial and showed little regard for the Politbureau as a collectivity, but this is not entirely true. Certainly, he tended to be arbitrary when he believed he was right and others simply did not understand his ideas. But his apparent disregard for the rest of the leadership stemmed from another reason altogether.

Throughout the period before 1976 the Politbureau contained an individual, Hoang Van Hoan, whom Le Duan wanted to get rid of, but could not. Firstly, Hoang Van Hoan was a veteran Politbureau member who could not be pushed aside. In terms of hierarchy and prestige within the Party, there had been a time when he was not inferior to Le Duan. Secondly, Hoang Van Hoan was close to China, which was at that time very important to Vietnam in its struggle against the Americans. Prior to the liberation of the south, a breakdown in relations with China would have created too many difficulties for Vietnam. Thus Hoang Van Hoan remained in the Politbureau, essentially for reasons of detente with China.

Beginning with the fall of Khruschev in 1963, Le Duan had changed his attitude towards the Soviet Union which he had previously regarded as the centre of revisionism. The improvement in relations culminated with Kosygin's visit to Hanoi in 1967. Le Duan also understood that the intentions of Mao Zedong towards Vietnam were dubious. Mao had once told him, in a phrase that later became famous, that 'a short handled broom cannot sweep far', which meant that the Vietnamese were weak and should not have too large ambitions. So Le Duan maintained a wary attitude towards China, while acknowledging Vietnam's need for Chinese aid in the war. Hoang Van Hoan therefore kept his position in the Politbureau. However, this also meant that any views expressed at Politbureau meetings would be reported straight away to the Chinese. Consequently, Le Duan did not like Politbureau meetings and, when he needed to call one, he was compelled to employ an elaborate strategem. In order to avoid inviting Hoang Van Hoan, Le Duan would first discover a reason why the General Secretary must send his Politbureau colleague to meet the Chinese leadership in order to discuss vital matters, in such a way that Hoan would not become suspicious. The Politbureau meeting would be called after the latter had departed for Beijing. Those were the conditions under which such meetings were normally held.

These subtle complexities of life in the Politbureau and of international relations are some of the reasons why it is unfair to describe Le Duan as dictatorial and arbitrary. By 1976, however, the task of liberating the south had been completed and he saw that he could remove the mask. At the Fourth Party Congress in late 1976, Hoang Van Hoan was removed from the Politbureau and after that the clashes with China began.[10]

Below the Politbureau was the Party Secretariat, the standing committee of the Central Committee, dealing with everyday problems in the nature of central Party administration. It could also act on behalf of the Politbureau to resolve problems normally of a non-strategic significance. However, it could also, on occasion, be used to issue more important decisions as a means of bypassing opposition or hesitation within the Politbureau. CT-100,[11] which legalised the contract system in agriculture in 1981, is a case in point.

The Central Committee (*Ban Chấp Hành Trung Ương* – literally Central Executive Committee), was elected by the Party Congress. For much of the period under consideration (i.e., from 1960 to 1976) the Central Committee was that elected by the Third Party Congress and comprised 47 members. Members were allocated responsibilities in key branches and localities: they were ministers or vice-ministers in key ministries, provincial Party secretaries in the most important provinces, ambassadors to the Soviet Union or China, or joined committees (*Ban*) belonging to the Party centre.

The structure of Party committees did not exactly copy the government structure, but grouped together some of the most important fields not necessarily coinciding with those covered by ministries. Whereas, for example, the Foreign Ministry was paralleled by the External Relations Committee of the Party, in the economic area there were fewer Party committees than ministries (replicating the Chinese model). Besides these, there were Committees for Propaganda, Science and Education, Culture and Ideology, Interior and, especially important, Party Organisation. In addition, another special committee, the Central Civil Administration Committee,[12] had special responsibility for Party organisation within the apparatus of government as well as the mass organisations.

By far the most important of these Party committees was the Central Party Organisation Committee, which was not only higher-ranking than the others, but embraced the whole apparatus of Party, central government, provincial and city authorities. This committee effectively made all personnel decisions for the state apparatus, including the National Assembly, government, Party, Central Committee, even membership of the Politbureau, provincial secretaries and chairmen.[13] For a long time it also decided who, among the cadres of the state machinery, could study or work abroad. In addition, the Organisation Committee played a paramount role in political security, in a sense standing above the Ministry of Interior. It could decide on arrests, discipline, promotions and diplomatic posts.[14]

To what extent the authority of this committee depended on the Party structure, or on the power and prestige of its chairman, Le Duc Tho, one of the leading Politbureau members, we can only speculate.[15] Since the power of appointment was one of the key instruments in ensuring implementation of Party policy, this in itself made the Organisation Committee very powerful. In practice, personnel questions depended on the relations between three key people – the General Secretary, the chairman of the Organisation Committee, and the Prime Minister in whose hands formal power over appointments in the government apparatus rested. Senior appointments involved considerable negotiation between the three. The Prime Minister could not, for example, remove a provincial leader if the latter had the support of either the General Secretary or chair of the Organisation Committee.

In the economic field, there were basically three key Party committees: the Central Agricultural Committee, the Central Industry Committee (by comparison, the government had five corresponding bodies: the ministries for Heavy Industry, Light Industry, Machinery and Metallurgy, Mining and Coal, and the General Department of Chemicals), and the Central Committee for Trade and Finance, responsible for banking, finance and domestic and foreign trade. Several ministries not considered of strategic importance, such as the Ministries for Fisheries, Irrigation and Forestry, had no parallel Party committee.

Party Committees were mainly responsible for research and analysis in their economic field and for developing policy proposals. Every policy towards a particular economic branch would normally first of all be sketched out by the relevant Party Committee. These Committees had both horizontal (with corresponding branches) and vertical relations. Vertical relations were with the Secretariat and Politbureau to which the committees reported. While they did not have executive powers or the authority to issue decrees, they played a very important role in preparation of decrees and in deciding the contents of Party resolutions to be put before meetings of the Central Committee or Politbureau. Only the decisions of the latter bodies and the Secretariat had 'legislative' authority.

An institution of the foremost importance in the Party was the Nguyen Ai Quoc Party School. Based in Hanoi, the school also had a provincial network charged with training and retraining of cadres in the whole state system comprising National Assembly, government, Party and mass organisations. High level cadres such as ministers, vice ministers and heads of mass organisations (who all must be Party members) were required periodically to attend classes of the Nguyen Ai

Quoc Party School. Those who could not pass the courses were seen as insufficiently capable of leadership roles in any organisation. Courses normally lasted for one or two years and the contents consisted of basic knowledge in the subjects like philosophy, economics, sociology, communism, Party history, law and management. Thus virtually all leading cadres from the lowest echelons up had received a set of basic precepts which contributed substantially to the development of a common outlook and common behavioural norms.

At the provincial level, the Party system was similar to that at the centre. First and foremost was the Party Secretary, the highest person in the province, ranking above the provincial Chairman who was normally also the Deputy Secretary. Beneath the Secretary was the provincial Standing Committee, usually including the Deputy Secretary as well as the provincial Vice Chairman. Below this again was the Provincial Committee apparatus, normally comprising provincial party members who were heads of sub-committees (as at the centre, there were Provincial Committees on Organisation, Agriculture, Industry, Science and Education, Propaganda), directors of departments in the local government, or chairmen and secretaries of important districts in the province. The provincial Party Committee always included the head of the Security Department, local head of the armed forces, head of the Office of the People's Committee and the provincial Vice Chairman.

Party organisation at the district level followed the same model as at the provincial level: Party Secretary, Standing Committee, District Committee, District sub-committees. The apparatus at the commune level, however, was simpler, as indeed it was on the government side. Each commune had a Party Secretary and Committee. The commune Chairman was often also the Party Secretary or Deputy Secretary, but was at least a member of the Party Committee. The system of sub-committees of the higher levels was too cumbersome at the commune level and normally individual Committee members took responsibility for an area of activity. If the commune had several cooperatives then the secretaries of the cooperative Party cells were usually also members of the commune committee.

RELATIONS BETWEEN THE PARTY AND STATE APPARATUS

First of all we need to distinguish between the concept of the state as it is used in Vietnam and the concept as understood in most western academic discourse. In the latter sense, the 'state' embraces the whole machinery of legislature, executive, bureaucracy, judiciary, armed forces and, the most important part in a one-party state like Vietnam, the Communist Party. The last mentioned is the body which decides policy as well as the institutional structure of the rest of the state apparatus. Its resolutions have the force of law. Thus it combines legislative, executive and, frequently, judicial powers. In Vietnamese usage, however, the state is clearly distinguished from the Party and includes only the legislature, government and organs belonging to the government (including the bureaucracy, judiciary, etc).[16] Other institutions which in reality carried out certain state functions in the period under consideration, such as mass organisations and cooperatives, were defined as 'non-state'. According to this definition, the state includes two basic structures – *legislature*, from the National Assembly down to local People's Councils, and *government*, from the central government down to the People's Committees in the provinces, districts and communes. In practice, since the legislative branch had few real powers, the term 'state' tends to refer to the government alone.

Official documents in Vietnam make the distinction between the Party and state and the two sets of institutions

are seen as different from each other. A basic principle
enunciated at the Fourth Party Congress (1976) by General
Secretary Le Duan was: 'The Party leads, the state manages
and the people are the masters'. For ease of discussion, we
use this conceptual distinction here. As we shall see, however,
the two systems cannot be separated in reality.

The principle of Party leadership was enshrined in the
resolutions of five-yearly Party Congresses,[17] which set out
the general line for the whole country to follow. Between
these Congresses, the Central Committee met every six months
on average, focusing on a particular topic at each session.
Resolutions of the Central Committee plena had the status of
law, although it was left up to the government to draft the
specific measures and organise the machinery to carry them
out. According to the principles of the Central Propaganda
organ of the Party, each time the Party (Congress or Central
Committee) carried a resolution, all cadres in the country
must study it. However, not all the details were made public.
Therefore, higher level cadres met in private for discussion
of the most secret aspects of the resolutions. Ordinary Party
members received less detailed information. By the time the
resolutions reached non-Party members, the content had
been much simplified and correspondingly less time was
needed for study. Non-publication of details of the resolutions
was an important method of Party control since it enabled
Party leaders to decide in an *ad hoc* fashion whether concrete
measures proposed by government officials were in accordance
with their desires or not. By the same token, government
officials needed to consult Party superiors in advance. A
further means of transmitting the line to state cadres was the
system of Nguyen Ai Quoc Party schools mentioned above.

Importantly from the point of view of implementation, the
Party had its own network within the state apparatus.
Foremost in this network was the Party group (*Đảng đoàn*),

the highest Party organisation within the ministries and usually including at least three people, the Minister and Vice Ministers and often department heads, who took on the responsibility for directly supervising implementation of the line within their ministry. One of the features of this period, compared with the 1950s, was that non-Party ministers had gradually disappeared.[18]

At the same time these Party groups provided a most important channel of communication between the bureaucracy and the Party centre. Feedback on organisational interests of a particular ministry could be transmitted to the relevant Party committee or articulated directly by members of the Central Committee and this served to provide the leadership with a gauge of the degree of acceptance and implementation of policies. However, what Shirk (1993: 69) calls the 'law of anticipated reactions' meant that, in presenting these interests, senior officials could not step too far out of line with the prevailing consensus within the Party centre. The culture of preserving Party consensus and the relative distance of other senior Party personnel from the problems experienced in a particular field, led to the practice of blaming lower level cadres for poor implementation of policies, or else blaming factors outside the central planning system itself when things went wrong. Fundamental criticism of policy direction, or of the model itself, would not be acceptable under normal circumstances. Thus the higher levels of leadership could remain in genuine ignorance of many of the real practical concerns of cadres at lower levels of the heirarchy. The implications for the reform process are that a ministry wanting to achieve change would have to ensure not only that its proposal was couched in terms according with what was understood by the majority as the 'socialist model', but that a sufficiently large number of other ministries were either supportive or neutral.[19] By meeting these two conditions, the leadership of a particular ministry could hope to persuade the Politbureau of the need for change.

Besides the Party groups, each state organisation contained a Party committee (*Đảng ủy*), that is the elected organisation of Party members within the state body. This committee's only functions were in relation to the internal work of the organisation to which it belonged and it had no direct relations with the Central Committee or responsibility for interpreting the Party line: these were the prerogative of the Party group. The Secretary of the Party Committee was usually head of an office or department in the Ministry and its relations with the Party centre were through the Civil Administration Committee and its Department of Cadre Organisation which accepted new members and approved candidates for elected positions.

Yet another institution linked the state organs to the Party leadership: the Central Party Organisation Committee dealt with the problem of personnel from the level of minister down and was responsible for oversight of the realisation of Party principles within the state organs. The corresponding Party committees also guided and coordinated with the ministries on questions of the Party line in relation to that ministry.

Thus there were many connections through which the Party could exercise its leadership over the state apparatus, as illustrated in Figure 3 overleaf.

RECIPROCALITY OF THE TWO SYSTEMS

One of the features of this diagram is that the state and Party systems, although technically separate from each other, were in reality interposed and overlapping.

First, there was the existence of two rules (Party and state) within one person. As noted above, most key cadres in the state organisations were simultaneously high ranking cadres in the Party. If they were introduced at a conference or

Figure 3: Links between state and Party Offices 1960–86

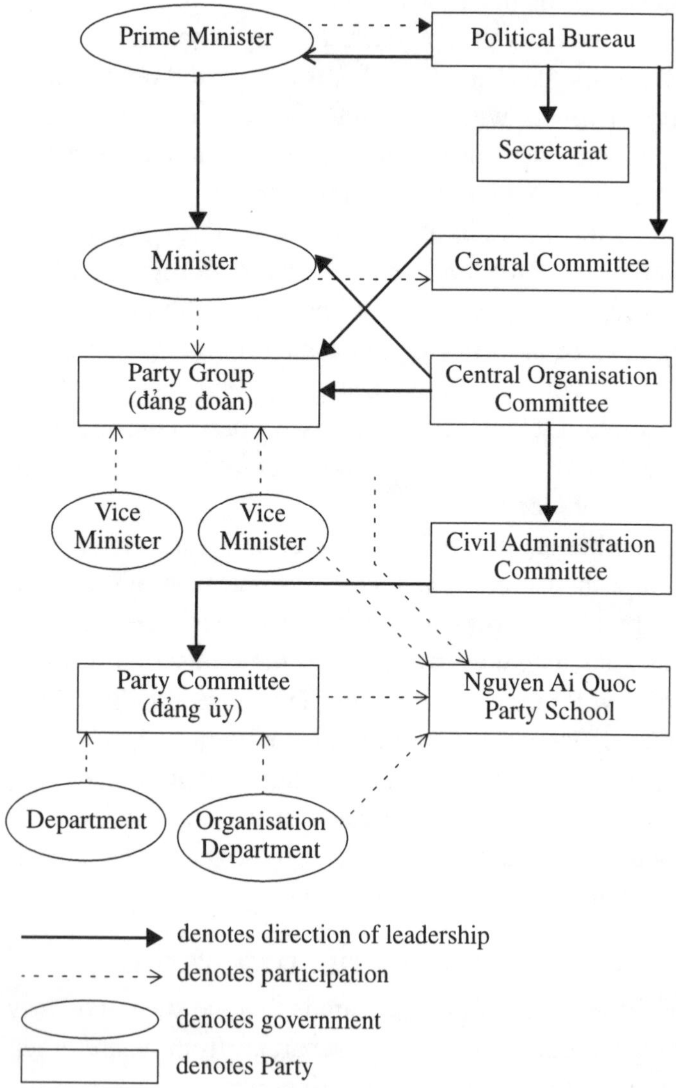

```
┌──────────────────┐        ┌──────────────────┐
│  Prime Minister  │·······>│ Political Bureau │
└──────────────────┘<───────└──────────────────┘
                                      │
                                      ▼
                              ┌──────────────┐
                              │ Secretariat  │
                              └──────────────┘

┌──────────────┐          ┌────────────────────┐
│   Minister   │·········>│ Central Committee  │
└──────────────┘          └────────────────────┘

┌──────────────────┐      ┌────────────────────┐
│   Party Group    │<─────│ Central Organisation│
│  (dảng đoàn)     │      │    Committee       │
└──────────────────┘      └────────────────────┘

┌──────────┐  ┌──────────┐    ┌────────────────────┐
│   Vice   │  │   Vice   │    │ Civil Administration│
│ Minister │  │ Minister │    │    Committee       │
└──────────┘  └──────────┘    └────────────────────┘

┌──────────────────┐      ┌────────────────────┐
│ Party Committee  │·····>│  Nguyen Ai Quoc    │
│  (dảng ủy)       │      │   Party School     │
└──────────────────┘      └────────────────────┘

┌────────────┐  ┌──────────────┐
│ Department │  │ Organisation │
│            │  │  Department  │
└────────────┘  └──────────────┘
```

─────────────▶ denotes direction of leadership

- - - - - - -▷ denotes participation

⬭ denotes government

▭ denotes Party

mentioned in the newspapers, however, the Party ranking of these individuals always came first. Prime Minister Pham Van Dong, for example, would be introduced as 'Comrade Pham Van Dong, Politbureau member and Prime Minister'.

Second, there was extensive and continual 'fluidity' of personnel movements between Party and state. An able, prestigious and experienced provincial Party secretary could be promoted to the position of minister at the centre, even Deputy Prime Minister or Prime Minister.[20] There were also less common cases of movement in the other direction, from state to Party.[21]

Thirdly there was close affinity and coordination of Party resolutions and government policy. State officials participated in the drafting of Party resolutions, especially those from branches related to the problem under discussion. In the case of the Eighth Resolution of the Central Committee (1985) on price-wage-currency reform, lengthy preparations were carried out by a joint sub-committee comprising Deputy Prime Ministers Tran Phuong and To Huu, the Chairmen of the State Bank and State Price Committee, and the Ministers of Finance, Domestic Trade, and Labour (all of whom of course were senior Party members). The resolution was drafted, therefore, not only by Party experts, but also by key members of the state apparatus. Thus, when the resolution was carried by the Party, there was also the expectation that it would accord with the demands of the state. At the same time, the 'law of anticipated reactions' ensured that policy emerging from such a process reflected the preferences of Party leaders. Thus there was a very tight reciprocality between the Party line and the state administration.

Besides this reciprocality, even if Party cadres in Vietnam did not work in the state, they remained on the payroll of the state. Party organs and cadres depended on payments from the state budget.[22] Expenditure by the Party on conferences, office buildings and newspapers was all paid for from the state budget. Special departments existed within the State Planning Committee and Ministry of Finance for material and budget allocations to the Party. Unlike the ministerial and provincial allocations, these were not submitted to the National Assembly for approval. Much the same situation exists today, despite the existence of Party business enterprises.

RELATIONS BETWEEN THE CENTRE AND LOCALITIES

Vietnam for long applied the principle of dual accountability (*song trùng trực thuộc*), derived from China.[23] According to this regime, each lower level organ was accountable, on the one hand, to the highest ranking person in their locality and, on the other hand, to the head of their branch at the centre. At the provincial level, for example, the Agricultural Department was both a part of the provincial People's Committee, accountable to the provincial chairman, and also a unit of the Ministry for Agriculture, accountable to the Minister. In principle, the dominant relationship was with the provincial chairman who signed all the relevant decrees and appointed or dismissed the director. On the other hand, all such appointments and dismissals must be approved by the Minister in charge of the relevant branch. In cases where the provincial Chairman and Minister could not agree, then one of the two could appeal to the Prime Minister. This system of horizontal and vertical relations was a means of guaranteeing central control because in reality the geographical relations were more sensitive than branch ones. In a given province, if all the directors of the different branches were accountable only to the centre, then there would be a lack of coordination between the ministries at the provincial level, leading to disarticulation. Moreover, criss-crossing lines of authority helps to prevent the formation of organised factions based on institutional interests.

In the model of dual accountability, the provincial chairman was more powerful than the minister, but the chairman was in turn directly responsible to the Prime Minister. In this way, it was supposed, the best interests of both the whole and the parts could be realised. If the chairman showed localist tendencies,[24] for example by ignoring the opinions of the central ministry, the minister could submit the matter to the Prime Minister for settlement. The outcome depended very much on the relationships between the individuals involved. While the Prime Minister was the nominal arbiter, the result also depended on the General Secretary and chair of the Organisation Committee. A provincial chairman, for example, who wished to avoid implementing a ministerial directive which was supported by the Prime Minister, could ask the local Party secretary to intervene on the province's behalf with the Party leaders in Hanoi. In some key instances in the 1980s, the most influential party personalities supported provincial leaders who had initiated reforms – indeed obtaining their acquiescence was a necessary precondition for continuing.[25] On other occasions, ministers could use similar means of overcoming the objections of provincial leaders.

Beside the personnel question, local organs were also responsible for implementing state policies within their jurisdiction. Government decrees, usually signed by the Minister of the relevant branch, applied to the whole country. As well, the local Departments distributed decrees issued by the provincial People's Committee, usually signed by the provincial chairman or vice chairman and dealing with the problems of either an individual branch in the locality, or the whole province.

At the district level, the horizontal and vertical relations were similar to those at the provincial. The head of a district agricultural committee depended both on the district chairman and on the head of the provincial Agriculture Department. However, at this level the ties to the provincial Department were stronger than those to the district chairman because the province was considered the basic administrative unit. The provincial chairman and heads of department usually directly supervised all economic, political and social activities in their province, so the district did not have the same independence from the province as the province had from the centre.

Below this, the structure of relations at the commune level was somewhat different, as shown in Figure 4.

At the commune level we do not find the system of dual accountability. Since there were no sections in charge of vertical branches like agriculture, industry, trade, finance, banking, etc., the machinery was correspondingly simpler, as described above. The commune People's Committee chairman depended for his authority on the District Chairman, while in economic activities, the base units (i.e., the cooperatives) in the commune were directly linked to the relevant district

Figure 4: Structure of relations between district and cooperatives

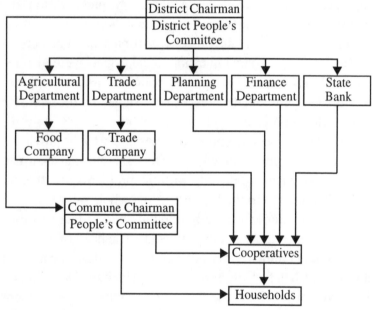

Notes to Figure 4

In domestic trade, foreign trade, banking and material supply there were three levels of companies known as: Level I companies, belonging to the centre; Level II companies, belonging to the province, and Level III companies, belonging to the district.

office. The district agricultural office, for example, was directly concerned with the agricultural development plan for all cooperatives in the district, working with them to distribute the annual production norms issued by the province. The district trade office was, at the same time, in charge of the 'level 3' companies of the district, such as the Foodstuffs company, the Agricultural Materials Company, the Foreign and Domestic Trade Companies which had direct links to the cooperatives under the plan.

The district thus related directly to the production base in the commune, irrespective of how many cooperatives the commune contained. Relations between the district and the commune authority, on the other hand, concerned administrative and territorial matters and were mainly dealt with by the respective chairmen of the two levels. Economic relations between the district and cooperatives only involved the commune People's Committee where disputes arose. In such cases the communal authorities would be called in as mediators, although the district authority remained the final arbiter.

Dual accountability at this level would have been unnecessary because the commune had no functions of economic governance. It was also a small unit whose machinery did not include the branches of the higher levels.

Relations between upper levels of the hierarchy and the co-operatives were formally different from those with the state enterprise sector. In the case of the collective economy the state did not directly allocate resources, but signed contracts with units which were regarded as formally independent. Relations between state and cooperative sectors were not seen simply in terms of relations between higher and lower levels: the important point here was the expression of relations between two different economic components – state and collective (or non-state). The commune Chairman was appointed by the district, but not the cooperative Chairman.

Nor did the commune Chairman have the power to appoint the cooperative management committee. It was the cooperative members who elected their production managers and representatives in relations with the outside world, that is, with the state. Relations between cooperatives and districts were seen as basically trading relations, even if this was 'trade' according to the central plan. Procurement targets were in fact coercive, and buying and selling were done according to state targets for quantity and price fixed in the production plan of the cooperative.[26]

In practice, the non-state character of the cooperatives was largely a fiction. Contracts were not freely agreed, but product mix, prices and quantities were essentially fixed by the planning authorities. Cooperatives were required to meet their procurement and tax obligations *before* assuring the basic subsistence of members or setting aside funds for welfare and investment, with the result that most cooperatives could not cover their real costs of production.[27] Private sector agriculture therefore became an essential means of supporting subsistence and of ensuring the long-term viability of the cooperative sector (Beresford 1985). The leadership of the cooperative, even if elected, was in the hands of the Party and, as such, responsible for implementing Party programs at the cooperative level. Moreover, under the Le Duan regime, the Party-state moved rather quickly to integrate the cooperatives more closely into the state-run economy.[28]

For most of the period the majority of cooperatives were basically production organisations and the administrative unit was the commune. However, some cooperatives organised child care, kindergartens, dispensaries, public works, Uncle Ho fishponds, sport, entertainment and religious facilities. Thus although the commune People's Committee was the main locus of this type of work, those cooperatives which were seen as the flag bearers of the cooperative movement had begun to take on the character of state authority. During the high point of cooperative development, in the latter half of the 1960s and early 1970s, the commune People's Committee began to be eclipsed. Cooperatives were already shouldering a large proportion of the work of local government: mobilisation for work on irrigation, village roads and tree planting, organisation of cultural life and morale, security, recruitment for the army and welfare. Considered in the light of the developmental trend of the model, Party ideology foresaw an increase in the role of state power at the cooperative level. The construction of high level cooperatives as precursors to cooperatives on a district-wide scale was part of this orientation. In the thinking of Le Duan, future cooperatives would take the form of people's power at the base level, the most thorough expression of 'collective mastery of the working people'. Working people would organise their own production and choose representatives to arrange all questions of economic, cultural and social life. However, Vietnam was still very far from realising this dream and in the meantime the cooperatives would have more of the character of production units than administration. The commune People's Committee would continue to play the role of the local authority.[29]

In functional terms then, the cooperative in Vietnam, prior to the period of the (CT-)'100 contracts' in the 1980s, had not gone very far along the road of becoming an economic-administrative unit. It was still far from the People's Commune model. Moreover, under the system of contracting to households, the cooperatives' role in economic and social governance has been much reduced. As is now the case with state enterprise workers, farmers' relations with the state apparatus are normally no longer mediated by the cooperative which has tended to become a mere service company for farm households. Since its state-like character has diminished, it may eventually evolve as a genuine cooperative organisation. The authority of the commune People's Committee as the basic administrative unit has been correspondingly enhanced.

THE DECISION-MAKING PROCESS

Decision-making in relation to the economy can be conceived of at several different levels: broad programmatic decisions which set the basic framework within which economic actors operate; strategic decisions affecting the medium- to long-term direction of particular sectors; shorter-term decisions affecting the macro management of the economy or of particular sectors within it; and, finally, the day-to-day decisions of economic actors (individuals or organisations) in response to the signals they receive from the wider context. It is far more difficult to achieve change in programs and strategies since they are likely to involve large numbers of interests and the breaking down of political alliances formed to put them in place. Any system operating under normal conditions (reasonable economic stability) is unlikely to produce pressure for large-scale changes.

In the context of Vietnam between 1960 and 1986 we can include in the 'programmatic' category those basic principles which were more or less commonly adhered to among all socialist countries after the 1920s – central planning, public and collective ownership of the means of production, distribution according to labour productivity and the achievement of rapid industrialisation through giving priority to heavy industrial development. Given Vietnam's rather dependent relations with the socialist bloc, especially the Soviet Union and China, these basic principles could scarcely be questioned before the mid-1980s when it became clear that changes underway in the Soviet Union itself would soon lead to fundamental transformation of Vietnam's relations with that country. It was not until 1988, two years after the rise of

Gorbachev, that one of the present authors was able to publish in *Nhân Dân* an article critical of the central planning system itself and openly drawing attention to the taboo which had hitherto surrounded discussion of the subject (Dang Phong 1988).

Variations in the 'socialist model' applied to different countries can therefore be explained by decisions belonging to the second category mentioned above. Among these we can include, in the case of Vietnam, the methods and scope of agricultural collectivisation, the policy of building districts into 'economic fortresses', the structure and rate of industrial investment. Most of the decisions in this category are strongly associated with the authority and prestige of Le Duan.

In the third category we can include decisions linked to implementation of the broader strategic ideas, concerning particular projects, for example, the structure of prices, or the selection of 'pilot models' as exemplars of the way in which collectivisation and industrialisation should be carried out. Here the imprint of the General Secretary is also very evident, although medium-term macro management of the economy was, as we shall see, an area in which local initiative, by ministries, provinces or lower-level localities, could also provide input into the national policy making process.

The final category includes decisions by local actors on concrete implementation of decisions emanating from above. In this area there was actually a rather wide scope for local decision-making, in the degree of enthusiasm with which policies were implemented, in the ability to re-interpret policy and through outright contravention of the letter of the law. That such scope existed throughout the period is evident from the frequent high level policy discussions on how to achieve better implementation of strategic and medium-term policy decisions, particularly in relation to the agriculture sector.[30] By the late 1970s, however, the negative reaction of most southern farmers to the government's collectivisation program combined with a series of external shocks caused by the renewal of war with China and Democratic Kampuchea, massive reductions in external assistance from the USA, China and the Soviet Union, and the impending application of much higher international trade prices with CMEA, led to conditions of recurring economic crises. In such a context, local economic actors responded by 'breaking the fences' established by the central planning system. Widespread existence of foot-dragging by localities, establishment of illegal check-points taxing trade, diversion of state-supplied goods onto the free market, decisions by local authorities to allow purchasing of farm products at prices above the official price, the spread of household contracts within the cooperative system, both assisted in the restoration of equilibrium and began to compel changes in strategic and medium-term decisions.

Between 1960 and 1976, the overriding concern, shared by the population of the DRV as a whole, to achieve national unity, tended to allow the political leadership to ignore systemic flaws which might otherwise have produced strong social tensions. Those day-to-day decisions by economic actors which were not in accord with the broader program of 'socialist construction' could be absorbed or deflected without real danger to the system because of the large amounts of Soviet and Chinese aid flowing into the country and easing shortages. Only after the restoration of peace, unification with the large market-oriented economy of the south, and the diminution of foreign aid, did these contradictions begin to emerge sharply enough for significant numbers within the political leadership to begin the process of questioning, first the strategic and then the programmatic aspects of the socialist model which the Party had attempted to construct since the late 1950s.

THE ROLE OF LEADING PARTY PERSONALITIES

Within the Party, the key figure in economic decision-making was the General Secretary. Almost all important changes in Vietnam and almost all the basic economic institutions, at the very least had his strong support and at most were directly inspired by him. Although agricultural collectives and industrial planning were standard socialist institutions, applied in different formats across the socialist world, the Vietnamese see these as primarily the work of the then General Secretary, Le Duan. What they mean by this is that Le Duan was the individual chiefly responsible for over-coming objections, for using his power and prestige to push through the necessary measures and for the particular form that they took in Vietnam. Ultimately, Le Duan can also be held responsible for the economic reform process. Without his encouragement and endorsement of experiments being undertaken at lower levels, the reform could not have pro-ceeded. In short, the General Secretary's authorship of eco-nomic measures consisted largely of his ability to decide, not only the direction of change, but the pace and detailed content within a broad framework laid down by Party consensus on the shape of the 'transition to socialism'. The General Secretary's power was enormous, but it was not absolute and, as we shall see, the Politbureau, as the collective body closest to him, and others also contributed to drawing up these programs.

Within the Politbureau, the pervasive influence of the General Secretary is evident even in cases where he kept in the background. A case in point is the criticism of the agricultural contract system in Vinh Phuc in 1968 launched by Politbureau member and National Assembly President, Truong Chinh.[31] Le Duan appears not to have been in sympathy with the severity of the criticism of the provincial leadership, although he did not oppose it. Nevertheless, precisely because Le Duan did not express a view, it was widely understood that he disagreed with the criticism. So, despite being criticised, Kim Ngoc, the provincial leader responsible for the contract system, was able to continue as Secretary of the province. In fact his power was increased when the province was merged with Phu Tho. Not only that, but a modified form of the system was permitted to continue.[32]

The Vinh Phuc case was a rare one. In most cases, other Politbureau members tended not to take independent initiatives, but to leave this field to the General Secretary. Nevertheless, the incident highlights the constraints on the power of a single individual. In spite of his disagreement with the criticism of Kim Ngoc, Le Duan was not able or willing to contradict the prevailing consensus within the Party centre in favour of a more orthodox application of the collective system and more centralised control over the economy.

A number of different factors can be used to explain the power of Le Duan during this period, of which one element was his prestige (*uy tín*). Prestige, which in Vietnam attaches more to the individual rather than to the position, is an important concept in Vietnamese political discourse. Where does prestige come from? Obviously, it is not innate to the individual, although intelligence, knowledge and talent may be prerequisites. One method of acquiring prestige would appear to be the ability to build vertical and horizontal political alliances – both acquiring the approval and patronage of someone higher up and garnering the support of one's peers – which enable one to move up the hierarchy and exhibit one's talents. Of these two methods, patronage would appear to be the most important in the early stages of a career, but the closer one moves to the top, the more important it becomes to create wider circles of support, especially since one's patron is likely to feel threatened by a protege who rises too fast or shows too much independence of thought. Since open political competition is not deemed acceptable, one of the chief methods of building alliances is to come up with a policy innovation which appeals to a broad section of the Party leadership. Once prestige is attained, it appears to take on a life of its own and becomes, in itself, an obstacle to potential rivals. However, it is by no means the sole prerequisite for the exercise of power and, with the regularisation of Vietnamese politics today, the incidence of power stemming from prestige, as in the case of many early revolutionary leaders, is much reduced.

In the case of Le Duan, the prestige which he gained early on appears to stem from his strategy for liberating the southern region. After the signing of the Geneva Accords, Le Duan remained in the south for two years, experiencing the hardships of Viet Minh cadres there and carrying out a thorough investigation of the situation. He returned to the north armed with a strategic plan for liberating the south through armed struggle. But it was not until the fifteenth Central Committee plenum held in January 1959, that he was able to persuade the Party centre that this would be the most reliable means to success. By that time, something of an impasse existed. The previous strategy of reunification of the country by peaceful means was clearly not working and, in reality, the Viet Minh in the south was on the verge of extinction, under the impact of Ngo Dinh Diem's repression. With strong backing from the southerners, Le Duan was therefore able to convince the majority that his new strategy was needed. In the following year, he was elected General Secretary. Later on, after the success of his strategy in 1975, his prestige reached its apex and his position became virtually unassailable.

Nevertheless, he also paid attention to the need to listen to views differing from his own. Within the Party and state apparatus, there were democratic and frank debates which often convinced the General Secretary to change his opinion.[33] He was in the habit of putting aside a considerable amount of time for discussions with his advisors and for meeting ministers to discuss the minutiae of their problems. He listened seriously, but had a caustic tongue and, when he could not be persuaded, subordinates had no choice but to implement his wishes.

Some of Le Duan's regular advisers were an important influence on his thinking.[34] For example, economists ultimately convinced him on the question of importing large Soviet tractors for the mechanisation of Vietnamese agriculture. Another example relates to the argument for cutting extensive investment during the 1976–80 Five-Year Plan. Le Duan was a person of large aspirations who wanted to push the development of the country quickly towards industrialisation and large-scale production. This desire had been one of the basic elements shaping the Five-Year Plan. But it soon became apparent that the capacity to fulfil the plan did not exist. The planners proposed the reduction of investment, abrogating some industrial construction targets and strengthening some of the smaller programs compared to the initial plan. Le Duan argued with fire for his own position, but ultimately conceded the point.

Expert advisors and ministers were also frequently used by the General Secretary to draft his speeches, a method which, despite the 'law of anticipated reactions', provided an opportunity for subordinates to have a direct input into the policy-making process.

Similarly, the localities often provided material which fed into the thinking of the top leaders. In the 1970s, for example, Dinh Cong cooperative in Thanh Hoa played a key part in forming Le Duan's ideas on large scale cooperative agriculture. The initiative of Quyen Luu district in Nghe An province on expanding the scale of the basic accounting unit to the district level, gave rise to the idea of building the districts into 'economic fortresses'. The local leader was promoted to Provincial Secretary. By the time of the 1979 Sixth Plenum, however, such experiments began to be considered utopian errors and the General Secretary began to look more favourably upon reformist experiments.[35]

Contacts with the leaders of other socialist countries and study tours also played an important role. Bulgarian large-scale agro-industrial complexes (APK), for example, influenced Le Duan's thinking on large-scale agricultural cooperatives and building the district into a unit embracing agriculture, industry, transport and communications. The Korean experience in military-style regulation of labour and living conditions also attracted him for a while. However, a study group, led by the director of the Institute of Economics, Tran Phuong, visited Korea in 1968 and recommended strongly against it, so the idea was abandoned. By the late 1970s, however, deterioration of relations with China, the only other country which was reforming its system in a fundamental way, meant that this source was no longer available. After the death of Brezhnev in 1982, Soviet advisory teams also began to be less frequent visitors, but at the same time tended to be internally divided on the question of reform.[36] Individual Soviet experts who were critical of the system in their own country were more likely to be in touch with lower ranking officials in Vietnam, but no doubt some of their ideas did filter up to the top.

Thus while the sources of advice and input into the decision-making process of top leaders like Le Duan were fairly narrowly confined, they provided a means of obtaining an overview of acceptance of policy and success of implementation. However, it was not an altogether efficient means since access to the General Secretary depended in large part on personal relations, while very few advisers were prepared to ignore the 'law of anticipated reactions'. Information not in accordance with his views was therefore likely to be filtered out at an early stage in the transmission process – a key factor which led to the isolation of top leaders from everyday reality and their slowness to change their views.

Among the basic ideas developed by Le Duan and those around him were the various strategies employed in agricultural collectivisation, rapid industrialisation, the district policy, and the idea of 'collective mastery' which he propounded at the Fourth Party Congress in 1976. This last, however, was something that even those closest to him did not clearly understand. For many years, the concept of 'collective mastery' was debated all over the country, but could never be precisely distinguished from Lenin's 'socialist democracy'. Conceptual imprecision provided scope for a lot of 'interpretation' at the lower levels, as we shall see, and therefore formed a useful device for maintaining broad legitimacy of the program favoured by the Party leaders.

One of the chief weapons the General Secretary could use was his power over personnel appointments.[37] Moreover, if he wished to avoid creating enemies, he could move people to positions of equal or even higher rank, but where they would no longer have authority in relation to centrally important questions. Periodic reorganisations of the government apparatus could also be used for the same purpose, to overcome institutional opposition to a particular set of measures. As mentioned above (p. 39), this method was used to promote the reform process from 1980 onwards. Thus the direction and pace of reform ultimately depended on the views of the General Secretary and the Politbureau.

Provinces operated in a similar way. The person who played the role of key decision-maker was the provincial Secretary, while the People's Committee Chairman basically played a co-ordinating role. There were few cases in which the Secretary

Source: The newspaper, *Lao Động*

"ĐẦY TỚ" LÀM SAI
"ÔNG CHỦ" CHỊU HẬU QUẢ

Tranh: VĂN   DANH   NHO

'The "Servant" makes mistakes, the "Master" bears the consequences.'

and Chairman disagreed, but where this became serious then the Central Party Organisation Committee would resolve the issue by personnel measures, moving one of the two elsewhere. This acted as an incentive for the provincial Secretary and Chairman to coordinate their work. While the Party Secretary was technically responsible only for Party work, in practice he participated directly in economic management and administration. The Provincial Secretary had the authority to issue direct orders to key provincial organisations, which in any case were run by Party members. The situation of the province therefore depended to a very large extent on the ability and ideas of the Party Secretary. In reality, from the 1960s through to the 1980s, the relative stagnation or progress of a province and its achievements in reform depended very much on the role of this person.

If we consider the evolution of this period, we find that the provinces leading the reform were all provinces with a Secretary who dared to think and dared to act. The contracts in Vinh Phuc were the work of the local Party Secretary, Kim Ngoc, and established by Decree 68-MQ/TU of 10 September 1966. Implementation of contracts in Haiphong was the initiative of City Secretary Doan Duy Thanh, set out in Decree 24-MQ/TU of 27 June 1980. The spread of market prices to the whole province and for all goods in Long An province in 1980 was implemented by the Provincial Secretary, Nguyen Van Chinh, and a group of his expert staff. The dynamism and creativeness of Ho Chi Minh City at the beginning of the 1980s was linked to the reputation of the then Party Secretary, Nguyen Van Linh.

In the localities, only the Party Secretary could lead reform measures, primarily because of his authority over all the important organisations in the province. His opinions carried weight with the local government, enterprises, branches, cadres and the people. Without the power and prestige of the local Party secretary behind them, it would be difficult for any branch or locality to implement any new and unusual ideas: 'fence-breaking' experiments could not survive without this support. As well, the provincial Secretary played a very important role in winning sympathy and support of the higher level leadership which would only accept bold reforms at the lower levels on condition that the head of the provincial Party organisation bore responsibility. Indeed, the ability of local leaders to implement unorthodox measures depended critically on whether support was forthcoming from the General Secretary and chair of the Organisation Committee. Usually the prestige of the Provincial or City Secretary was a key factor in getting a sympathetic response from the centre. Thus in the localities where the Party Secretary's ability and prestige were well known at both higher and lower levels, the conditions for reform were more favourable.

Prestige was not the only factor, however. The context in which local reformist experiments took place is also important. Vinh Phuc is a case in point. During the 1960s, the broad consensus within the Party favoured the orthodox application of the agricultural collectivisation model. It was wartime, Soviet and Chinese aid were available to offset the effects of shortages and, to the extent that a crisis of the system was perceived to exist, it lay in the threat posed by the Americans. Relative to the rest of the Party, then, and despite whatever prestige he might have had, Kim Ngoc went too far out on a limb and found himself criticised. Whether from his own inclination or not, he had failed to achieve the sort of high-level support which was necessary to the survival of such experiments. At that time, the dominant view in the Party was that problems with the collective system were not immanent to the system itself.

By the early 1980s, however, the context had changed. The war was over and efforts to tighten up collective management according to the orthodox model had repeatedly proved fruitless. In an atmosphere of economic crisis, the top leaders were more ready to look favourably on experiments which might provide a way out of the impasse. Moreover, as early as 1976 Le Duan had caused the promotion of a number of reform-minded individuals from positions in the political periphery (as advisors, for example) to more powerful jobs in the Central Committee and ministries. The climate favouring reformist experiments was altogether more favourable and it was in this context that initiatives taken by Party secretaries in Haiphong, Long An, An Giang and Ho Chi Minh City were successful. Once these experiments were seen to succeed, they tended to spread. Ultimately, measures begun in the provinces were applied by the centre to the whole country. The provincial leaders who had first nurtured them, gained in prestige and were often promoted to central level positions, as in the case of Nguyen Van Linh who became General Secretary, the Secretary of Haiphong who ultimately became a Deputy Prime Minister and the Secretary of Long An who became Chairman of the Vietnamese Peasants' Association.

The actual power of ministers also depended partly on ability and prestige, and on their position on the Central Committee or Political Bureau. However, even these individuals sometimes lacked real authority. Vo Nguyen Giap, for example, when he was Defence Minister, was compelled to cede most of the decision-making power to a handful of (not necessarily the highest ranking) generals who had the confidence of the General Secretary. Moreover, although the Minister of the Interior was a Politbureau member, the most important and secret issues were handled by the Organisation Committee (headed by Le Duc Tho). Non-Party ministers, that is those who had remained for a while from Ho Chi Minh's government, had insufficient actual power to run their ministries. They might have been able persons, but they also well understood their real political strength and worked as if they were expert advisors to the real minister, namely one of the vice ministers who was also a Central Committee member.

LEGISLATION AND IMPLEMENTATION

In most political systems legislatures can initiate legislation, but rarely do so. In the majority of cases the initiative comes from the government. In Western democracies the main function of the legislature is to scrutinise and amend legislation emanating from the government and this appears to have been the case also in the early period of the DRV. With the 'partification' of the state, however, legislation was initiated through the resolutions and directives of the Party, though these were not technically referred to as 'laws'. In

Source: The newspaper, *Lao Động*

TRANH: CHUỒNG

LĐ 93 11/4

Capacity (*năng lực*) is too small compared to responsibility (*nhiệm vụ*) but with the aid of an umbrella or two (namely a ranking Party official) things can be done.

reality, however, Party resolutions and directives were a form of 'pre-legislation' or 'supra-legislation'

The Political Bureau, most typically the General Secretary, developed the basic ideas. These ideas did not merely reflect the subjective goals of the leadership, but were generated in a variety of ways, most immediately from close advisers, from the localities and branches, or from the experience and advice of other socialist countries. Nevertheless, the basic ideas of the General Secretary and Politbureau shaped the specific content of Party Congress and Central Committee discussions. While Party Congresses were concerned with long-term strategies, Central Committee plena were held approximately every six months and discussed more immediate and concrete problems prepared for them by the Secretariat. In fact, the Central Committee plena, like the legislature, mainly scrutinised and amended the prepared resolutions. These resolutions of both the Party Congress and Central Committee formed the skeleton of national legislation. All branches and levels were required to study and implement correctly the ideas in these resolutions.

The process of formal regulation and legislation was carried out by the government and National Assembly normally following the Central Committee meetings. Party committees worked with the relevant government bodies to prepare the necessary documents. In the case of personnel changes, which were a key method of ensuring implementation of Party resolutions, the Party Organisation Committee would work with the Office of the National Assembly for this purpose. When the General Secretary had the idea to build the district level into an 'economic fortress', he found it necessary to merge a number of provinces, to widen the scale of the province and it was the National Assembly which issued the official decree merging the provinces. The basic content of changes to all laws and the Constitution emanated from the

Party centre and the only real role of both government and Assembly was to systematise them in the form of legislation. The National Assembly did not conduct any real debates: at its meetings, which were short and infrequent, representatives gave their unanimous approval without actually knowing the details of the decrees they were passing.[38] This was the most stifling period for the National Assembly and very different from both the earlier period and the post-*đổi mới* National Assembly. Similarly, the government apparatus lacked sufficient authority. Prime Minister Pham Van Dong often lamented that he neither sufficiently understood key issues nor had the power to decide, particularly on the question of appointments which were formally his prerogative.

This method of formulating decisions had the advantage of giving the Party dominance over the policy-making process. However, as a method of achieving tight control, there were also some defects and loopholes in the system.

Firstly, although Central Committee resolutions were Party documents and carried the force of law, they were secret. Dissemination of the resolutions for study by cadres therefore discriminated between different levels – the highest levels receiving the full details, but lower levels only a general outline. For non-Party members and ordinary people the information content threw an even dimmer light. In the areas of external relations and security discussion was internal and highly secretive. Party resolutions on relations with China and the Soviet Union, for example, were not published in *Nhân Dân* at all.

Secondly, Party resolutions and orders bore the imprint of the personal ideas of the General Secretary and Politbureau members, particularly before 1979. Given the process of filtering of information about popular acceptance of various programs, there was little way in which the laws could be shaped by the power and interest of the wider society. Instead the leadership tended to take up ideas thrown up in discussions with experts, local officials or from various visits and researches in fraternal socialist countries. Even if the personal ideas of the leaders also aimed to reflect the interests of the country as a whole, the rather narrow basis on which they were formulated meant that their application could adversely affect the majority – the program of building up districts as 'economic fortresses', for example, or the highly voluntarist targets of the 1976–80 Five-Year Plan.

Thirdly, Party resolutions did not go into the specifics of legislation and execution. Due to the theoretical and propagandistic style of writing, they contained a lot of vague ideas which could be understood only with difficulty. For example the economic slogan of the Third Party Congress (1960), to 'Give rational priority to heavy industry, while simultaneously strongly developing light industry and agriculture', was oft repeated in resolutions of the Central Committee. Over the years, however, no one could explain precisely to what level heavy industry should be developed and to what level light industry or agriculture should be developed. Between 'rational priority' and 'strongly developed' which should be given the greater weight? In the state plans, therefore, these ideas could be given quite different weights without violating the principle of implementing the Party resolution.

Here we have a clue to the considerable scope for flexibility in the decision-making process which allowed lower level authorities to interpret the content of resolutions without appearing to alter the basic contents and thrust.

Immediately following the Central Committee meeting, a series of conferences would be organised in order to explain, interpret and discuss the implementation of Party resolutions. This was an important area in which scope for policy development by the lower levels existed. After the Sixth Plenum in 1979, for example, Deputy Prime Minister To Huu organised a conference of provincial leaders and ministers to discuss the resolution. Many of these would have attended the Central Committee meeting itself. But without violating the letter of the resolution, the conference produced a more radical interpretation of the decisions made at the Plenum than had been apparent in Le Duan's closing speech. Similar conferences were always held within branches and localities as well, allowing very different weights to be given to various aspects of the resolutions according to local conditions.

This meant that a much wider range of people than the Party centre had the opportunity to participate in the policy making process. Moreover, working conferences designed to implement the Party line could provide higher ranking officials with important feedback from the lower levels about the impact certain policies were having. This is not to say that such meetings invariably produced critical views, as the invitation list could be controlled by the organisers and the 'law of anticipated reactions' would also be at work among those whose jobs depended on the continued approval of their superiors. However, given that Party leaders basically determined which groups in society should have a voice in the policy-making process, it was in their interest to delegate a certain amount of authority in order to ensure that policy ultimately was acceptable to those groups and would be implemented properly by them.

In the provinces and districts, the lack of precision in Party resolutions shaped the way provincial leaders worked towards practical implemention. Acute and able local leaders could, by skilful propaganda and reports to the centre on the outstanding achievements of units in their province, draw attention to their province, thereby increasing their own prestige. For this purpose, provinces used the method of creating 'pilot models', which became a very widely used method of giving some concrete expression to vaguely worded Party resolutions.

The basic idea behind the 'pilot model' was a ready-made application of the Party resolution which would show its superiority in enhancing the material wealth of the population and become a pattern for the whole country to follow.

The 'pilots' were usually selected on the basis of genuine achievements in improving the material standard of their members through collective activities – construction and repair of irrigation works, for example – and were then promoted as models for the collectivisation or industrialisation program of the rest of the country. In the 1970s, for example, Dinh Cong cooperative in Thanh Hoa province and Quyen Luu district in Nghe An province were, as mentioned above (p. 64), influential on Le Duan's strategic thinking. Leaders of such models received promotion, newspapers wrote frequent reports on them and groups from all over the country went to inspect them.[39]

However, the very process of becoming 'models' led to a certain falseness and unreality: they were given special conditions, so that they never lacked material supplies, capital or finance for health and cultural services. The Ministry of Culture would supply free musical instruments to establish an enterprise band and the Ministry of Health would build a health centre or a dispensary for the model enterprise – all to impress visitors. If the helping hand of the centre had been omitted, then it would have been virtually impossible for these cooperatives to sustain the necessary standards to remain 'models'. But for budgetary reasons, only a few such models could be set up: there was no capacity to multiply them across the whole country. Moreover, the models needed to be changed fairly often, due to the need for frequent policy changes as existing models proved inapplicable to the wider context. After five or six years a different 'pilot model' would be selected.

In a comparative perspective we can see some changes in the 'pilot models' between this period and the next. During the 1960s and 1970s, the 'pilot model', even if its original development had come from genuinely cooperative actions of its members (as in the case of Dinh Cong), became something implanted and supported from outside the economic unit and no longer corresponding to the internal needs and capacities of that unit. Thus they had no inner vitality. They were like cut flowers in a vase, having no roots and only surviving because of the water in the vase. Eventually they withered.

During the early stages of *đổi mới*, however, and earlier if we look at agricultural contracts in Vinh Phuc and other provinces in the late 1960s and early 1970s, the 'models' took on an opposite nature and significance. They were not planned according to any theory or resolution, but arose spontaneously from the day-to-day needs of the population and, if nurtured by their localities, were able to take root and show greater vitality than the earlier models because they had an economic raison d'etre. The only thing lacking was political approval because they were contrary to the traditional model. Therefore, they could only survive if defended by the local leadership and, by implication, some of those higher up. While these models were initially seen as dangerous weeds in the socialist garden, later on, like many weeds, they were cultivated and allowed to multiply because of their real benefits.

Cases were common enough of documents being issued by provinces that were not accordance with those issued by the central ministries. In fact there were not only cases of contradiction between documents issued by provinces and ministries, but between the different ministerial branches. Within a single branch there could also be contradictory documents issued at different points in time. Such differences were normally resolved by means of Circular Letters (*Thông tư hướng dẫn*). Those issued by the provincial committee were normally used to explain and guide the execution of central directives. As their aim was to assist application within the specific circumstances of the province, they could often contain distortions of the central policy. For example in 1979, the then Ministry of Public Security (i.e., the Ministry of the Interior) issued a Circular decreeing that, in order to be able to buy petrol, all motorbike users must have papers showing that they were cadres or civil servants. At the time, the shortage of petrol was critical and the decree was intended to prevent use for non-official purposes.[40] But the document put out by the Ho Chi Minh City Committee, while not declaring its opposition to the Circular of the Public Security Ministry, stated that in the actual circumstances of the City, many people needed to use their motor bikes to meet the demands of everyday life and the measure would temporarily not be applied. In this case 'the writ of the king yielded to the village' (*phép vua đã thua lệ làng*). In substance, however, it was not the *phép vua*, but only a Circular Letter of a ministry.

The higher the source of a decree, however, the greater the potential for damage to the career of local politicians from this kind of behaviour. Thus, in the case of a decree signed by the Prime Minister, localities might adopt a less bold approach and simply drag their feet in implementing it. A typical example was the attempt to halt the flow of goods onto the market in the localities. The central government issued many Circulars demanding the abolition of this situation, but in practice the localities maintained checkpoints, searched people's luggage and caused inconvenience to travellers on the roads and railways over a long period. Though the checkpoints might be suppressed temporarily, they always reappeared because they had emerged in response to the real needs of local finance. In 1989 the Politbureau itself issued an order to abolish the controls and guarantee the circulation of goods throughout the country. Because the local leaders could not circumvent an order of the Politbureau without incurring damage to their political life and status, the restriction on movement of goods did then reduce considerably.

In terms of the decision-making process, both the new type of 'model' and the 'foot-dragging' process represented the interests of those who, throughout the long period of Le Duan's stewardship, had been effectively disenfranchised. They reflected not only an economic crisis of the centrally planned economy, but a political crisis in which a disjunction between the articulation of the 'national interest' by the top leadership and the articulation of local interests by lower level officials had emerged. As Party leaders increasingly recognised this disjunction, tolerance of experimentation at the lower levels increased and, through the activities of individuals in the political periphery (advisors, local Party secretaries, etc.) were gradually fed into the policy process. In the 1980s, then, one could say that there was a shift in the composition of the groups to whom Party leaders looked for the development of policy initiatives.

In summary, the decision-making process was conceived of as top down, with the General Secretary and Political Bureau taking all the most important decisions and the government and legislative structures merely implementing. However, at the lower levels there was some scope for authority within the broad framework laid down by the Party leaders. This flexibility within the system amounted to an ability of branch and locality leaders to develop policy through their interpretation of orders from higher up. In some cases these policy developments received the active approval from the Party centre, but in others the local leaders skated on the edge of acceptability and legality. Nevertheless, this flexibility and relative pluralism in the system was one of the factors enabling experimentation to take place in the 1970s and ultimately contributed to the demise of the planned economy.

NOTES

1. General Secretary Truong Chinh took personal responsibility and resigned.

2. Vietnam Workers' Party, Resolution of Central Committee Plenum no. 14, in CPV(1995: 119)

3. He died in 1969 at the age of 79.

4. In the early 1980s this was renamed the Council of Ministers (*Hội Đồng Bộ Trưởng*). Under the 1992 Constitution collective responsibility was dropped in favour of cabinet-style government with a Prime Minister at the head. The cabinet is referred to as the Government (*Chính Phủ*).

5. The longest serving incumbents of the chairmanship were Nguyen Duy Trinh and Le Thanh Nghi.

6. In this area Vietnam seems to have followed the Chinese rather than the Soviet model (Shirk 1993: 59–61).

7. This method could, of course, be used to achieve the converse result.

8. In the 1986 merger, for example, the former Minister for Domestic Trade became chairman of the Union of Artisan Cooperatives.

9. There were rare cases when this was not so: Nguyen Van Linh, for example, became Secretary of Ho Chi Minh City, although he had lost his Politbureau position. Hanoi has also had Party Secretaries who were not in the Politbureau, like Nguyen Van Tran and Nguyen Lam, although these two were members of the Party Secretariat.

10. This history was related by one of Le Duan's close confidants, although it will never be found in any of the official documents.

11. Party Secretariat Order no. 100 'The reform of contract work and the expansion of output contracts with groups of workers and individual workers in agricultural cooperatives', 13 January 1981.

12. *Ban Dân Chính Trung Ương*. The name is not easily translatable. *Dân* refers to organisations which were formally non-governmental, while *Chính* refers to government authorities.

13. Appointments, etc., at lower levels were the responsibility of the Organisation Committee of the level above. Since it was the most important Party committee at each level, the chairman would normally be Deputy Secretary of the locality.

14. In his 'Open Letter' to the Politbureau of 1981, Nguyen Khac Vien complained that the Committee had 'encroached on the

powers of government' (cited in *Far Eastern Economic Review*, 26 February 1982).

15. The question is probably a chicken-and-egg one: Le Duc Tho's prestige probably originated independently of his role in the Organisation Committee, thus enhancing the prestige of that Committee, but his chairmanship of it also provided him with a powerful opportunity to exercise patronage (and its reverse), thereby enhancing his own prestige and that of his clients.

16. Since there is no separation of powers it is not necessary to include other organs such as the judiciary, since these are simply arms of the government (though technically subordinate to the National Assembly). Under *đổi mới*, however, there has been some attempt to bring about a separation of powers.

17. In reality, they were not held during wartime. The Fourth Party Congress did not convene until 1976.

18. Earlier, if Ministers were not Party members (mostly those who had worked in Ho Chi Minh's government), a member of the Party centre worked as Vice Minister and was simultaneously Secretary of the Party Group. For example, when Phan Anh was Minister for Foreign Trade, his Vice Minister was Ly Ban, a member of the Central Committee and Secretary of the Party Group. Hoang Minh Giam, sometime Minister for Culture was also not a Party member, so Central Committee member Ha Huy Giap was appointed Vice Minister and Secretary of the Party Group. Other ministries which followed this model at one time or another were the Ministry of Education under Nguyen Van Nguyen, and the Ministry of Agriculture under Nghiem Xuan Yen.

19. See Beresford and Fforde (1996) for a discussion of the politics of reform, particularly as it related to the Ministry of Domestic Trade in the 1980s.

20. Doan Duy Thanh, for example, went from Secretary of Haiphong prior to 1985 to Minister of Commerce (combining the old Domestic and Foreign Trade ministries) and then Deputy Prime Minister. Hoang Minh Thang, Secretary of Quang Nam-Da Nang became Minister for Commerce. Hoang Qui, former Secretary of Vinh Phu province, became Minister of Finance at the beginning of the 1980s. Vo Van Kiet was Secretary of Ho Chi Minh City before 1982 when he became Deputy Prime Minister and Chairman of the SPC. Mai Chi Tho, another former Secretary of Ho Chi Minh City was appointed

after 1986 as Politbureau member and Minister of Interior.

21. Nguyen Dinh Tu, for example, went from Minister for Higher Education to the Central Science and Education Committee. In 1980, because of the need to move the head of the Party Agriculture Committee, Ngo Duy Dong, who was unsympathetic to the contract system, Vo Thuc Dong who had been Minister for Agriculture replaced him. Truong Quang Duoc went from head of the Forestry Department to head of Customs, then Chairman of Haiphong People's Committee and later Secretary of Quang Nam-Da Nang. Mai Thuc Lan, former head of the Budget and Planning Committee of the National Assembly, was also promoted to Secretary of Quang Nam-Da Nang.

22. *Nhân Dân*, the Party newspaper, for example, was sold for 0.05 dong, below the cost of the paper it was printed on which was, in turn, sold at a low fixed price. The level of subsidy for *Nhân Dân* was worked out by the Ministry of Finance and State Price Committee.

23. In Chinese, *shuangchong lingdao*.

24. The Kim Ngoc incident mentioned on pp. 61–62 could be seen as 'localism' in the context of the time. Therefore Le Duan could not openly oppose Truong Chinh if he saw the principle of centralism as being more important at the time than the need for reform.

25. When the provincial leaders of Long An wanted to violate the fixed price system in 1980, they first obtained the approval of Le Duc Tho, Le Duan and Nguyen Van Linh (who was then Party Secretary of Ho Chi Minh City), not of the Prime Minister.

26. Urban handicraft cooperatives were in a similar position to agricultural ones, belonging for administrative purposes to the ward (*phường*) level of local authority. Their economic relations were directly with the district (*quận*) via the district companies and, as with the agricultural cooperatives, these relations were ones of compulsory purchase and sale. However, the obligations of the handicraft cooperatives were not as heavy as those of the agricultural cooperatives and had more of the character of trade, albeit at subsidised state prices. Since in the urban areas it was not possible to self-provide means of subsistence as in the countryside, members of these cooperatives, like state enterprise workers, also received supplies of rice, textiles and fuel.

27. Fforde (1989) contains a rather detailed discussion of the implications of this system for cooperative-state and cooperative-farmer relations.

28. The structure of official prices, for example, was at somewhat of a divergence from Stalin's insistence that trade between state and non-state entities should follow the law of value (Stalin 1952: 19–23).

29. State enterprises, by contrast had already taken on most of these non-production functions.

30. For example, the Central Committee plena in 1963–64 which discussed at length the problems of agricultural pricing and of domestic trade; the Thai Binh Agriculture Conference in 1974.

31. Vinh Phuc adopted a contract system similar to that which became widespread in the early 1980s.

32. Contracts existed in other provinces as well during the early 1970s (Kerkvliet 1995).

33. For example, the debate on liberation of the south already mentioned, that on the pace of collectivisation in the early 1960s, numerous debates about the problem of agricultural procurement and prices from the 1960s onwards and, above all, the debates about the direction of reform during the late 1970s and in the 1980s.

34. People like the agronomist Luong Dinh Cua, physicists Nguyen Dinh Tu, Nguyen Van Hieu and Vu Dinh Cu, and economists Tran Phuong and Doan Trong Truyen were invited to expound their ideas on agricultural development, science and technology, Marx's *Capital* and the results of their research trips to the socialist countries.

35. In 1979, the originator of the Quyen Luu experiment was promoted 'out of the way' to the Ministry of Food which, in 1980, was then merged with the Ministry of Domestic Trade under the reformist leadership of Tran Phuong.

36. A group of three Soviet academics who visited Long An in 1983 were split two to one in favour of the reforms in the province.

37. Ngo Duy Dong, head of the Party Agriculture Committee, who did not agree with the contract system introduced in 1981, was replaced by Vo Thuc Dong, former Minister for Agriculture. This also happened to To Duy, Chairman of the State Price Committee,

who persisted with the old subsidised price system when the leadership wanted it changed. He was moved to another job and replaced by a more progressive individual, Doan Trong Truyen. Dang Viet Chau, Minister for Foreign Trade in the 1970s, was an experienced veteran revolutionary and the person responsible for the design of the whole system of subsidised foreign trade. In 1980, faced with the demands of renovation in the economic mechanism, Le Duan replaced him with Le Khac.

38. The Chinese have a saying which echoes Le Duan's slogan of 'the Party leads, the state manages and the people are the masters', but conveys a rather different meaning: 'The party committee waves its hand, the government goes to work, the people's congress standing committee votes and the people's consultative congress claps' (cited in Shirk 1993: 57).

39. During one three-month period, Dinh Cong cooperative received an average of 500 visitors a day. It of course could not afford to accommodate such an influx without substantial additional resources.

40. The accompanying slogan was 'Value petrol as if it were blood' (*Quý xăng như máu*).

3

The High Reform Period

1986–Present

Once the process of 'fence-breaking' by lower levels became established during the 1980s, the economy began to undergo rapid institutional change. The scope of market relations expanded and, in response, the lines of state authority began to shift. This transformation emerged most clearly after 1986, as the system underwent a gradual change towards 'Statisation' (using the term in the Vietnamese sense) of political power and a simultaneous transformation of the state's role in the economy. This tendency was manifested in a number of different ways: firstly, a relative retreat by the Party from direct involvement in economic life; secondly, increasing power and volume of work for the government and legislature; and thirdly, a shift towards 'arms length' economic management, through macroeconomic instruments and 'rule by law' (as opposed to direct personal intervention by leading personalities).

The Communist Party had suffered a series of blows to its prestige and authority as a result of consecutive failures of policy in the second half of the 1970s. As it had claimed all the credit for leadership in every sphere and for organising every triumph, public opinion tended, according to the same principle, to hold the Party machinery, particularly the General Secretary, responsible when economic crisis and falling standards of living emerged. Le Duan's prestige had deservedly risen to its greatest height during 1975–76, immediately after the anti-American war. But perhaps the very enjoyment of this prestige encouraged him to press for economic programs which, the longer they went on, the more they were seen to be mistaken. Accordingly, his prestige began to fall early in the 1980s and, as his own authority declined, so did that of the Party as a whole. Semi-public complaints by Pham Van Dong, that as Prime Minister he had no real authority, reflected the view of the government apparatus about Party encroachment on its sphere of responsibility. The General Secretary himself had begun to search for new solutions, promoting a number of reformers to key positions in the late 1970s and endorsing some of the market-oriented experiments taking place. However, he was unable openly to repudiate his earlier position and it was left to others, especially his possible successors, to proffer alternative policies and programs. During 1983–84, Truong Chinh, then President of the National Assembly, promoted a popular slogan 'take the people as the root' (lấy dân làm gốc), which also reflected a widespread view that the the Party's methods of economic management were arbitrary and undemocratic.

Meanwhile, the domestic economy had begun to boom, the market mechanism was becoming more entrenched and, as a result, the influence on everyday life of decrees from above was reduced. There was a growing need for transparent and consistent laws and regulations to replace the system of extra-legal and supra-legal orders and decrees.

Conflict with China over the overseas Chinese in 1978 and the Chinese offensive of early 1979 greatly reduced the influence of the Maoist model in Vietnam, even if only superficially.[1] China had begun its own economic reforms at about the same time, but, in Vietnam, from 1979 onwards, nobody dared openly suggest studying the experiences of the 'reactionary clique' in Beijing.[2] In reality, however, a lot of information about the Chinese reforms fell into the hands of Vietnamese researchers who realised it could provide effective medicine for Vietnam's own illness (precisely because a large part of the illness had been spread from China). In the Party's Institute for Research on Marxism-Leninism, from about 1983 onwards, the section specialising on China research began to collect and translate all kinds of documents and analyses, from Hong Kong, the Soviet Union and other countries, on the Chinese reforms. Ideas such as 'feeling one's way across the river' and increasing the purchasing price of agricultural products according to the formula '7/3 reversed' (meaning reversal of procurement of 70 per cent of agricultural goods at fixed prices and 30 per cent at market prices, so that 70 per cent could be purchased at market prices) were raised by many Vietnamese around 1983–84. In one internal discussion on the Chinese reforms attended by one of the present authors in 1984, around 40 per cent of the opinions expressed seemed to support the Chinese method of proceeding. But it was only after 1986 that the Chinese reforms could be more widely discussed.

Probably the strongest external influence was from the Soviet Union and Eastern Europe: *perestroika* and *glasnost* of Gorbachev, the rise of a non-Party Prime Minister in Hungary, elections in Poland, crisis in Czechoslovakia, the collapse of the Berlin wall, the death of Ceaucescu. All these events and movements aroused a strong inclination for reorganisation in Vietnam: taking the 'people as the root' and increasing the role of law and government. But it was only after the rise of Gorbachev in the revolutionary homeland that such ideas could be widely and openly discussed. Earlier movements, such as Solidarity in Poland, had little influence on Vietnamese thinking as long as fundamental change in the USSR itself seemed a remote possibility.

In such an environment, the renovation of social life which took place had two key aspects, economic reform and the democratisation of power.

TRANSFORMATION OF THE ROLE AND FUNCTION OF THE PARTY

While the Party has remained a very powerful institution, its 'governmental' functions have been much reduced. Party organs no longer directly participate in the work of the government and the Party machinery has become correspondingly smaller. At the central level, all the former Committees in charge of economic areas have been merged into a single Economic Committee. Moreover, compared with the size and scope of the former committees, the merged Committee is smaller. Its task is basically research and advice and it no longer plays the role of a parallel ministry. Partly this reflects the increasing complexity of the market economy and much larger role of the private sector. Partly it is the result of the transformation of the economic mechanism: management is no longer carried out by state directives, but by indirect levers (incentives and sanctions). The flows of information which enabled Party committees to intervene directly, no longer exist. While the Party economic organs continue to research and develop desirable policy orientations, these no longer have the all-embracing impact of earlier times, largely because businesses pay more attention to the legal situation and the state of the market than to the political line. The Party groups too were replaced, in 1986, by Committees of Party Workers (*ban cán sự*), an adaptation to *đổi mới* which leaves them in a less powerful position than their predecessors.

One of the effects of this change is that many Party cadres have transferred to the government apparatus where there are more opportunities to obtain prestige and influence. Some Party organs have even been transformed into government bodies, for example the Nguyen Ai Quoc Party School. Although it remains a Party body in reality, it has been transformed legally into a National Institute, basically for convenience in relations with foreign counterpart organisations.

At present the Party centre only has nine Committees:

- The *Central Party Organisation Committee* still has the job of organising cadres for the whole Party and government machinery, but its functions and power have been greatly reduced. It no longer has the final decision on appointing and dismissing ministers and vice ministers, but works as the personnel office for the Party centre, principally the Politbureau, in deploying and training cadres. The personnel function in relation to the government apparatus has been transferred to an organ of the Government, namely the Government Committee on Organisation and Personnel (GCOP). Curtailment of the function and authority of the Central Organisation Committee was also in notable part linked to the illness and departure from the Politbureau, in 1986 after the Sixth Party Congress, of Le Duc Tho.

- The *Central Economic Committee*, as mentioned above, conducts research on theoretical problems and economic principles and no longer directly runs economic branches.

- The *Central Committee for Internal Affairs* deals with problems of security and defence, but also only through research and gathering data as a staff section of the Politbureau.

- The *Central Science and Education Committee* conducts research on trends in science and education.

- The *Committee on Culture and Ideology* conducts research on problems of literature, art and intellectuals. Perhaps, among all the Party committees, it is one of the most authoritative, simply because the area of which it takes care is the one in which the Government has no real power.

- The *Central Committee for External Affairs* conducts research and provides information to the Party centre on the international situation and the external strategy of the Party.

- The *Central Control Commission* is responsible for investigating errors and breaches of Party discipline – for example, the now numerous cases of corruption – and deciding the punishment to be handed down. In practice this Commission's authority is not as great as in earlier times. Its main work is considering petitions concerning discipline of Party members within ministries and provinces, the majority being low level and often trifling matters. For example, in the earlier period the Control Commission had to concern itself with the question of sexual relations between Party members and others, under the heading of *hủ hoá* (a Chinese word imported to Vietnam in the 1950s which can be translated as 'moral turpitude').[3] In the last decade, the conception of such degeneracy has changed alongside the increased personal freedoms associated with *đổi mới* (including greater sexual freedom and acceptance of pop music and new clothing fashions). Remaining crimes of concern to the Commission are those such as using one's authority to acquire above-standard housing, factionalism in the office, revenge against opponents, coveting money, goods, or office vehicles. Important political cases, such as that of Tran Xuan Bach in 1990 and Nguyen Ha Phan in 1996,[4] are resolved by the Politbureau.

- The *Central Financial Management Committee* is the internal office managing the Party's assets and organising the businesses which fund the Party organs. Obviously these funds provide only a small part of the expenditure on the Party apparatus, nearly all of which still comes from the state budget.

- The *Central Committee for Popular Mobilisation* is concerned with liaison with the mass organisations, the Trade Union, Peasants' Association, Women's Union, various scientific and technical associations, and the Fatherland Front – in other words, all the non-Party and non-governmental organisations. It is not a very important committee as, in practice, the above-mentioned organisations have a very formal character, at least in relation to the decision-making process, and their leaders are usually figureheads. Normally one of the less powerful Politbureau members heads the Committee; for example, Hoang Quoc Viet after the Third Party Congress in 1960, Nguyen Van Linh from 1979–82 and Pham The Duyet since the Eighth Party Congress (1996).

Another aspect of the Party's relative withdrawal from the sphere of government is the fact that after the Sixth Party Congress in 1986, although the majority of ministers, especially those in the key positions, were Central Committee members, several were not. After the Eighth Party Congress in 1996, however, a number of ministers who had failed to gain Central Committee positions were replaced by Central Committee members, suggesting a desire by the Party to regain the initiative.

INCREASING ROLE AND POWER OF THE LEGISLATURE AND GOVERNMENT

The National Assembly has gradually gained more real power and been able to give more substance to its work. Its debates have become livelier and representatives are no longer required to agree on everything. It has gained more real decision-making power in areas which used to be the preserve of the Politbureau. For example, in recent years the National Assembly has played the role of the final arbiter in certain controversial areas such as the price of electricity,[5] the construction of the 500 kv power line, and in choosing important investment projects. Since *đổi mới*, if the General Secretary proposes an idea, it is by no means certain that it will be easily accepted by the National Assembly, especially if there is no obvious backing from the relevant government bodies. The individual prestige of the leaders is not lesser, but the social power has increased. Government and Party leaders are compelled to take more notice of an Assembly which has been escaping slowly from its former spirit of passivity. Meetings of the National Assembly have become more frequent and normally run for three or four weeks (compared with a week in earlier times) due to the increased volume of work.

Since 1994, the Prime Minister has asked some government ministers not to run for the National Assembly, the idea being gradually to create a separation of legislature and executive and overcome the situation known as 'both player and referee' (vừa đá bóng vừa thôi còi).[6]

However, to say that the independence and power of the Assembly has increased is not to say that it is something beyond the Party or standing in opposition to it. In any case the President of the National Assembly is in the Politbureau, indeed one of its most important members. Moreover, candidates for election are normally approved by the Fatherland Front, itself an organisation led by the Party and, unlike the pre-1955 Assembly, there are no other parties represented.[7] So the National Assembly is very much led by the Communist Party as far as the political line is concerned. However, one might say that there has been a shift towards democratisation because the elected representatives now play a stronger role in interpretation and development of Party policy, a role which was previously confined to the government and Party machinery. Moreover, the National Assembly meeting in late 1996 demanded a stronger say in ministerial appointments. These developments mean that the governmental process is open to wider public scrutiny than before.

While at the central level the Assembly has clearly increased its influence, the role of People's Councils at the lower levels remains rather formal and weak. Real authority still belongs to the Party and government apparatus. Like the National Assembly, these People's Councils meet twice a year to review the implementation of central Party resolutions and economic plans (for the first six months if it is a mid-year meeting, or for the whole year if it is an end-of-year meeting). The People's Committee chairman of the relevant level reads a report and this is followed by discussion and questions. Sometimes these discussions can become heated, but they are normally restricted to such local issues as public hygiene, social evils or living standards of public employees. After the debate comes the explanation by the local authority of its position and the recording of questions in order to demonstrate that the opinions of the people's representatives have been taken into account. Finally the Party leaders present their views and instructions, normally according to the format of 'welcoming and highly appreciating the contributions of the representatives, affirming the democratic character of the proceedings and reminding the local authorities to pay heed to the people's representatives.' These formalities are followed by tea and dinner where everybody happily shakes hands. It is not that the People's Councils lack significance, but their authority is greatly restricted by three features.

First, as representatives from the base units (enterprises, cooperatives) and lower levels of government, they have insufficient resources and information to decide serious problems. They lack the resources, and therefore the independence, to carry out proper investigations, so their observations and criticisms can be based only on a partial and shallow view. More importantly, the People's Councils lack budgetary powers. The great majority of budget allocations are decided at the central level and merely implemented at the local level.

Thus, while local representatives may find many inadequacies in the services for which they are in principle responsible, they do not have the power to allocate extra funds. It frequently happens that government functionaries, knowing that nothing better can be achieved, nevertheless make heated criticisms in their role as people's representatives.

Second, the absence of genuine opposition can be explained by the lack of independence from the Party-state apparatus of the representatives, even when they are not Party members. Although they stand for election in the name of the people, candidates of People's Council positions cannot, in reality, normally hold political attitudes contrary to the Party and government if they want to be pre-selected. Where independent candidates do venture to stand, they usually fail to get elected. This is one of the key features of Vietnamese political culture.

Third, there is undeniably a certain degree of consensuality among the various institutions in Vietnamese society which makes it different from the plural democracies. While the Communist Party certainly cannot satisfy the aspirations of all groups in society, it is difficult for anyone to deny its historical role in the destiny of the nation. Moreover, more than one generation of Vietnamese have committed their flesh and bones to the survival of the regime. The Party thus retains a broad-based legitimacy and, despite local differences, it is unlikely that we would see the development of any large-scale opposition to it in the medium term. Even more so in the localities, large numbers of people see the CPV as their flesh and blood. Although it was the Vietnamese periphery which initiated fence-breaking and reform, it also remains the stronghold of Party and of socialist ideology, even if, in their daily activities, provincial and district officials often succumb to corruption. This is one of the paradoxes of Vietnamese society, as of many others. The more unreasonable aspects of this paradox, however, have the capacity to lead in future to major conflicts containing the possibility of regime collapse.

Because a lot of the functions previously carried out by the Party have now been delegated to the government, the size and power of the government machinery has increased. Gradually, and most of all under Vo Van Kiet's premiership, the government ministries have become the most powerful bodies in the economic sphere. Ministers are accountable to the Prime Minister (himself a senior Politbureau member) rather than directly to other Party leaders. Although they still, of course, normally belong to the Central Committee, ministers tend to adopt a more technocratic approach to their work. There is increased scope for the open expression of an institutional or sectoral view which, as mentioned above (p. 48), is an important mechanism for ensuring that the Party line is acceptable to its constituency.[8] The relative openness of the process also serves to ensure that a wider constituency is involved, even if it does not have direct access to the decision-makers and, in relation to Party decisions and many government documents (for example, the budget statistics), there remains a large amount of secrecy.

As a result of this shift in the policy-making arena as well as the need to introduce laws and regulations adapted to management of a market economy, people have observed that, during the period since the Seventh Party Congress in 1991, the government has done more work than it did in the whole period of Pham Van Dong's premiership. The government is no longer a secondary office of the Party centre.

The arbitrary nature of government has also begun to be reduced. In the past ministers and provincial chairmen had the power to allocate resources by virtue of their signature on a piece of paper. Their signatures were a powerful bargaining tool in relations with various organisations and brought them personal benefit. Today, the power of the signature is gradually disappearing as resource allocation mechanisms take on more of the character of commercial transactions governed by law. While heads of organisations had the power to give ('selling as giving'), then they had the power to take ('buying as robbing'). However, if the state has nothing to give according to its norms of supply and at low prices, then it cannot take from the economic units in an arbitrary way as before.

Public administration reform has been largely directed towards moving the country gradually towards 'rule by law'. However, this does not constitute the 'rule of law': rather it means that instead of vaguely worded Party resolutions which provided scope for varying interpretation by lower levels, the government now intends to supervise the drafting of detailed prescriptions and proscriptions which should be clear enough for all officials to follow. The aim is therefore to provide more transparency and uniformity in the application and enforcement of decisions. However, the general line decided by the Party still constitutes an orientation which the government seriously and strictly adheres to. Rule by law thus constitutes a 'regularisation'[9] of the political process rather than a democratisation. But this regularisation is an important step in institutionalising government processes, in replacing internal and secret relations with public and formal ones, thus opening them to greater public scrutiny and, potentially, to further democratisation.

The changes to the Vietnamese political system which have taken place since the 1980s do not constitute a return to the pre-1955 model. It is no longer wartime and there is no longer a figure like Ho Chi Minh with supreme authority over all areas of Party and government activity. The over-riding concerns of both sets of institutions are with economic and social, rather than defence and security problems, in the context of a more diverse and internationally-oriented socio-economic system than existed in the first decade after inde-

This cartoon expresses a cynical view of public administration reform, implying that the merger of ministries has produced no streamlining of the system. (**Source:** The newspaper, *Lao Động*)

pendence. Moreover, these are concerns which have arisen not only from the advent of peace, but from the insurmountable difficulties to which the central planning system gave rise. The massive changes which have taken place in the economic and social structure as a result of the impasse reached by the 'traditional' socialist system, have necessitated changes in the way the state apparatus functions. Many of these changes remain undeclared since the prestige of particular leaders and of the regime itself is at stake. Nevertheless the broad consensus around the reform process and the relative stability of the political system, indicate that the latter is capable of responding to pressures from below.

NOTES

1. For example, the slogan 'the Party leads in all areas' was an interpretation of Mao's 'the Party is the commander-in-chief'. The system of political commissars, which Lenin had imposed in the

Russian civil war, had been applied in China in the period after the war, not only in the army but throughout Chinese social institutions, and was copied in Vietnam.

2. In the 1980 Constitution, Vietnam affirmed that China was its lifelong enemy.

3. Ho Chi Minh provided a definition in his 'Letter to the People's Committees of Provinces, Districts and Villages' in October 1945: 'Hủ hoá is wanting to eat delicious food, wear beautiful clothes, live more and more luxuriously, be more and more romantic. Consider where the money comes from. It also means privatising public work, forgetting integrity and morality. Mr Committee Member goes by car, then Mrs Committee Member visits her friends and relatives also using the public car. Consider who bears the cost' (Ho Chi Minh 1970: 59).

4. In the first case a Politbureau member went as far as advocating political pluralism; the second, also a Politbureau member, was charged with betrayal to the French of a large number of his comrades during the 1950s in the south. At the time of his arrest shortly before the Eighth Party Congress in 1996, the latter was considered a possible candidate for Prime Minister.

5. In the past the Politbureau decided the prices of rice, electricity, basic metals, cotton and fertilizer. The proposed price rise for electricity in 1995 was put to the National Assembly by the government and was widely thought to be opposed by at least one leading Politbureau member. When the vote came, there was only a 15 per cent majority in favour of the increase.

6. Note, however, that the separation of powers was not incorporated in the 1992 Constitution, despite some advocacy of it (Thayer 1993: 52).

7. The stipulation that all candidates are approved by the Front has been relaxed recently, but without very noticeable impact. See Carlyle Thayer (1993: 56–64) for details of recent electoral developments. In the 1997 general election, three self-selected candidates were elected.

8. In Vietnam, unlike China, the Party leadership has not depended on the army to maintain its power. Therefore a basically cooperative relationship between the Party centre and other social organisations is more important.

9. Carlyle Thayer used this term to describe the institutionalised process of generational transition within the Party leadership between 1951 and 1986, pointing out that as the economy and society had diversified and developed, representation of different groups and sectors in the Central Committee had correspondingly widened to include those not belonging to the original generation of revolutionary leaders (Thayer 1988: 177–193).

Concluding Remarks

In this small book we have tried to identify first of all the processes leading to the 'partification' of state power in Vietnam – the formation of a Party-state under the leadership and direction of the Communist Party. The ability of the Party to assume a pre-eminent role in the exercise of state power was based on a number of factors: the weakness of potential opposition at the time of the August Revolution, the capacity to forge national unity in the face of serious economic crisis and foreign aggression and, not least, the drift towards reliance on the Soviet Union and China under pressure of international circumstances.

Nearly a century of colonialism in Vietnam had severely disrupted Vietnamese society: it had materially and culturally impoverished the peasantry, changed the social organisation and balance of power in village communities, divided the numerically small intelligentsia and created a dependent and craven elite. But it had also created a new working class and, despite itself, introduced radical ideas of democracy and equality. During the revolutionary turmoil of 1945 and the subsquent resistance war, it was the Communist Party leadership alone which was able to appeal to both popular discontent among workers and peasants and their willingness to act against the sheer oppression of French colonialism. On the other hand, the non-Communist intelligentsia had clearly failed to ignite the fires of popular passion. Apart from those too compromised by their collaboration with the colonialists and those unwilling to accept the massive shift in social power implied by the Party programme, Vietnamese intellectuals therefore by and large committed themselves to working for the new state.

Thus the broad-based legitimacy gained in this period gave the Party-state the strength and momentum to extend its program of social and political transformation through the 1960s. Even if the interests of many individuals were hurt by this program, there was also great pride in the achievement of national sovereignty and a clear improvement in the average conditions of daily life compared with the colonial period. The prestige gained by the Communist leadership in the early revolutionary period both forestalled the development of interest-based opposition to Party rule and severely weakened the critical capacities of the intelligentsia. These tendencies were only strengthened by renewed foreign aggression in the 1960s.

At the same time, however, it is clear that in a diverse society like Vietnam, there always existed tensions between the perceptions and interests of different groups based on regions, branches, economic conditions and positions in the political and administrative hierarchy. Despite the institution-alisation of Party rule and ideology through such mechanisms as Party groups, the Party school, the role of the Central Organisation Committee and the 'supra-legal' status of Congress, Central Committee and Politbureau decisions, such differences necessitated flexibility in both the inter-pretation and implementation of decisions at lower levels of the hierarchy. As we have shown, in the absence of 'rule by law', both the vague wording of decisions and the importance of personal relations and prestige gave scope for participation in economic decision-making by leaders located in the 'political periphery'. Even at the peak of 'partification', the

Party-state had neither the political will nor the resources available to it to be able to impose the wishes of those at the centre in all spheres.

A degree of flexibility in the decision-making process did not reflect the existence of opposition to the regime. Rather, it was necessitated by the operation of the system of central planning under conditions of acute underdevelopment and repeated economic crises (at least some of which were brought about by American aggression and the vicissitudes of foreign aid). Fence-breaking activities and foot-dragging by enterprises, localities and individuals and the issuing of circulars guiding implementation which revised or even contradicted directions from the centre, were means by which serious economic imbalances could be at least partially rectified.

Meanwhile the capacity of the prestige of early Party leaders (like Ho Chi Minh, Vo Nguyen Giap, Pham Van Dong and Le Duan) to motivate the population to adhere to the programs laid out by new generations of leaders began to wane. Especially after the liberation of the South and the achievement of sovereignty over the entire national territory, people's attention focussed more strongly on economic issues. The ending of the national emergency produced the need to regenerate the Party's prestige and legitimacy on a new basis. That those further up the hierarchy understood this reality is demonstrated by their frequent acquiescence to fence-breaking activities, especially from the late 1970s onwards, as well as by the perpetual search for new policy solutions.

During 1979–81, the difficulties of absorbing the market economy of southern Vietnam, combined with a series of severe external shocks (loss of US aid to the south, loss of Chinese aid, war with China and Democratic Kampuchea, and a large increase in the prices of goods imported under

Soviet aid) exposed the weaknesses of the central planning system further. In the context of falling output and state procurement in all sectors, many leaders at the centre came to accept that renewed attempts to obliterate the free market would be counterproductive. From then on, the transformation of economic life, through the process which became known as *đổi mới*, was increasingly associated with a transformation of political relations in the country. Particularly since 1986, decentralisation of economic decision-making powers and the associated needs for increased market regulation and more transparency in the legal system have shifted both the balance of power and volume of work in the direction of the government and legislature.

We have described this political transformation as a process of 'Statisation'. It is a reflection of two tendencies at work within the Vietnamese state system. On the one hand, there is the increasing strength of society. People are materially better off, better educated and, due to the relative stability of social institutions, better organised. On the other hand, the national leadership can no longer rely on the prestige and legitimacy gained from its early revolutionary successes. Prestige now has to be won and re-won. Moreover, the tendency towards regularisation of the political process is an important step in institutionalising government processes, in replacing secret internal Party relations with public and formal ones, thus opening them to greater public scrutiny and, potentially, to further democratisation.

Despite the scale of the political changes so far, there are, of course, many continuities in the system of authority relations which exists today. The Communist Party remains the main influence on political life and continues to exercise considerable power in economic policy-making – chiefly through the appointment of senior Party members to key positions in the state apparatus. The organisational capacity

of the Communist Party gives it both the ability to dis-
organise any potential opposition and the necessary flexibility
to respond to changes occurring in society.

Over the past five decades, the Party has invested all of its
prestige in the three goals of achieving national sovereignty,
industrialising and modernising the country, and creating a
more equitable society. Under the circumstances of almost
continuous war between 1946 and 1980, a remarkable amount
was achieved. However, the failure to climb out of poverty
has meant that for the foreseeable future the main goal will
be that of industrialisation and modernisation. The desire for
prosperity drives the Party no less than the population as a
whole. At the same time, despite the temptations and realities
of corruption, the present generation of Party leaders have
not forgotten that they spent most of their lives striving for
independence and socialism.

It is perhaps the question of independence which poses the
most difficult problem today. Integration of the Vietnamese
economy into the world market system threatens the ability
of the Vietnamese state to direct the development process in
a way that it has not experienced before. Western multilateral
institutions and investors complain that government procedures
are inefficient, that commercial law is not sufficiently
transparent and fair, and that not enough emphasis is given to
the development of the private sector. Foreign and local
investors alike, largely ignore government attempts to over-
ride market-based decisions and push resources into socio-
economic development projects such as regional development
or heavy industrial enterprises. A perception, by foreign
private investors, in particular that the Party and government
had failed to adequately address these questions led to a large
reduction in foreign capital inflow during 1997. Coming on
top of this, the likely impact of the financial crisis which hit
the Western Pacific Rim economies during 1997 remains, at

the time of writing, a controversial topic of debate in Vietnam. These are serious problems and it seems likely that, as in the past when confronted with the need for adaptation and change, the Vietnamese state system will undergo a further period of transformation.

Bibliography

Beresford, Melanie 1985. 'Household and Collective in Viet-
    namese Agriculture', *Journal of Contemporary Asia*,
    15:1

—— 1988. *Vietnam: Politics, Economics and Society*, Pinter,
    London

Beresford, Melanie and Irene Nørlund 1995. 'Democracy and
    power in transitional one-party culture', paper presented
    to the NASEAS annual conference, *Political Culture
    in Southeast Asia*, Uppsala University, 1–3 September

Beresford, Melanie and Adam Fforde 1996. 'A methodology
    for understanding the process of economic reform in
    Vietnam: the case of domestic trade', *AVRP Working
    Papers* no. 2, Sydney

Công Báo (Government Gazette), various issues from 1945–96

CPV 1980. *50 Years of Activities of the Communist Party of
    Vietnam*, FLPH, Hanoi

—— 1995. *Lịch sử Đảng Cộng Sản Việt Nam*, Hanoi

Dang Phong 1988. 'Cái gía của lãnh phí va cái gía của tiết
    kiệm trong các kế hoạch kinh tế xã hội', *Nhân Dân*, 12
    August

Dang Phong 1991. 'Nhìn lại chăng dường kinh tế 45 năm
    qua', *Nghiên Cứu Kinh Tế*, no. 2

——— 1997. 'Road Map of the Vietnamese Economy: some turning points along the way', paper presented to the Euroviet III conference, Amsterdam, 2–4 July

Doan Trong Truyen and Pham Thanh Vinh 1966. *L'édification d'une économie nationale indépendante au Vietnam (1945–1965)*, Editions en Langues étrangères, Hanoi

Duiker, William J. 1995. *Vietnam: Revolution in Transition*, Westview, Boulder

Fforde, Adam 1989. *The Agrarian Question in North Vietnam*, M.E. Sharpe, New York

Gordon, Alec 1981. 'North Vietnam's collectivisation campaigns: class struggle, production and the "middle peasant"', *Journal of Contemporary Asia*, vol. 11

Guillaumat, P. 1938. 'L'industrie minérale de l'Indochine en 1937', *Bulletin économique de l'Indochine*, November–December

Ho Chi Minh 1970. *Vì độc lập tự do vì chủ nghĩa xã hội*, NXB Sự thật, Hanoi

——— 1994. *Hồ Chí Minh Biên Niên Tiển Sử*, vol. 4, NXB Chính Trị Quốc Gia, Hanoi

Honey P.J. 1962. *North Vietnam Today*, Praeger, New York

Huynh Kim Khanh 1982. *Vietnamese Communism 1925–1945*, Cornell University Press, Ithaca

Lê Văn Hiên 1995. *Nhật ky một bộ trưởng*, 2 vols, NXB Đà Nẵng

Moise, E.E. 1976. 'Land Reform and Land Reform Errors in North Vietnam', *Pacific Affairs*, vol. 49

Porter, Gareth 1993. *Vietnam: The Politics of Bureaucratic Socialism*. Ithaca: Cornell University Press

Shirk, Susan L. 1993. *The Political Logic of Economic Reform in China*, University of California Press, Berkeley

Stalin, J. 1952. *Economic Problems of Socialism in the U.S.S.R.*, FLPH, Moscow

Thai Quang Trung 1985. *Collective Leadership and Factionalism: An Essay on Ho Chi Minh's Legacy*, Institute of Southeast Asian Studies, Singapore

Thayer, Carlyle A. 1988. 'Regularization of Politics: Continuity and Change in the Party's Central Committee 1951–86' in David G. Marr and Christine P. White (eds), *Postwar Vietnam: Dilemmas in Socialist Development*, Cornell University, Southeast Asia Program, Ithaca

—— 1991. 'Renovation and Vietnamese Society: the changing role of government and administration', in Dean K. Forbes et al. (eds), *Đổi mới: Vietnam's* Renovation Policy and Performance, Australian National University, Political and Social Change Monograph no. 14, Canberra

—— 1993. 'Recent Political Developments: Constitutional Change and the 1992 Elections', in Carlyle A. Thayer and David G. Marr (eds), *Vietnam and the Rule of Law*, Australian National University, Political and Social Change Monograph no. 19, Canberra

Trần Phương (ed.) 1968. *Cách Mạng Ruộng Đất ở Việt Nam*, NXB Khoa Học Xã Hội, Hanoi

Turley, William S. 1980. *Vietnamese Communism in Comparative Perspective*, Westview, Boulder

Viện Sử Học 1990. *Việt Nam Sự Kiện 1945–1986*, NXB Khoa Học Xã Hội, Hanoi

VNTKKC 1997. *Việt Nam Thời Kỳ Kháng Chiến chống Pháp (1945–1954)*, NXB Văn hoá Thông tin, Hanoi

Vo Nguyen Giap 1964. *Dien Bien Phu*, FLPH, Hanoi

Vo Nhan Tri 1963. *Croissance économique de la République Democratique du Vietnam, Editions en Langues étrangères*, Hanoi

—— 1990. *Vietnamese Economic Policy since 1975*, ISEAS, Singapore and Allen & Unwin, Sydney

White, Christine P. 1983. 'Mass mobilization and ideological transformation in the Vietnamese land reform campaign', *Journal of Contemporary Asia*, vol. 13

Index

The Nordic Institute of Asian Studies (NIAS) is funded by the governments of Denmark, Finland, Iceland, Norway and Sweden via the Nordic Council of Ministers, and works to encourage and support Asian studies in the Nordic countries. In so doing, NIAS has published well in excess of one hundred books in the last three decades.

Nordic Council of Ministers